TWIN FLAMES

First published in 2026 by Wellfleet Press,
an imprint of The Quarto Group,
135 West 36th Street, 13th Floor,
New York, NY 10018, USA
(212) 779-4972
www.Quarto.com

EEA Representation, WTS Tax d.o.o.,
Žanova ulica 3, 4000 Kranj, Slovenia.
www.wts-tax.si

Wellfleet titles are also available at discount for retail, wholesale, promotional, and bulk purchase. For details, contact the Special Sales Manager by email at specialsales@quarto.com or by mail at The Quarto Group, Attn: Special Sales Manager, 100 Cummings Center Suite 265D, Beverly, MA 01915 USA.

10 9 8 7 6 5 4 3 2 1

ISBN: 978-1-57715-743-4

Digital edition published in 2026
eISBN: 978-1-57715-866-0

Library of Congress Control Number: 2025944601

Publisher: Rage Kindelsperger
Editorial Director: Erin Canning
Creative Director: Laura Drew
Managing Editor: Cara Donaldson
Editor: Natalie Butterfield
Cover and Interior Design: Ashley Prine/Tandem Books
Text: Stefanie Weiss

Printed in Huizhou City, Guangdong, China TT112025

IN FOCUS

TWIN FLAMES

Your Personal Guide

SABINA STRAUSS

wellfleet press

CONTENTS

INTRODUCTION

Relationships. Some say you can't live with 'em, and others say you can't live without 'em. They come in every possible shape, size, and configuration. But no matter how bonds between humans have been defined or how they have evolved over time, we're still developing the right language to describe our most profound partnerships: those soul-to-soul encounters that change our lives forever.

What Are Twin Flames?

Philosophers and theologians have grappled with the concept of the soul for centuries, and poets have longingly written about their soulmates for almost as long. Although the modern concept of Twin Flames was first popularized in the 1980s, it still has roots in ancient mythology; it echoes the Egyptian story of how the goddess Isis and her husband Osiris were split and reunited. Contemporary writers also often use the concepts of the divine feminine and divine masculine to describe Twin Flame connections, drawing on Tantra, Hindu cosmology, Egyptian cosmology, and Gnostic and Kabbalistic traditions, amalgamated into a New Age worldview. (More about the New Age movement in Chapter One.)

The internet has produced dozens of articles and countless Reddit threads about Twin Flames, especially in the years since the pandemic, when interest in this topic exploded. In simple terms, a Twin Flame relationship occurs between two people who each possess half of a single soul that was split at some point on its journey. These two halves are Twin Flames. When Twin Flames meet each other, the relationship they form can be one of the most intense, dramatic, and challenging relationships of those individuals' current lifetime. Sometimes, these relationships deliver incredibly intimate, pleasurable sex—the kind that people describe as "mind-blowing" or "the best sex of our lives." Sometimes Twin Flames form a platonic bond that is strong—perhaps even unbreakable—and deeply complex. These relationships are often rife with psychological triggers that change the two partners' lives forever.

When a Twin Flame soul sees its other half for the first time in this lifetime, it might be instantly plunged into the throes of love and longing. At least one half of the pair may experience profound desire, ambivalence, and often an obsession with understanding the nature of the relationship. (Often both partners experience this, although one member of the pair might be less willing to acknowledge it.)

Soulmates, Twin Flames, and Other Relationships

Whether we call our beloveds partner, boyfriend, girlfriend, husband, wife, bae, friend (with benefits), lover, or something else entirely, *something* initially drew us to them. And when these connections are particularly intense and overwhelming, we might not be able to articulate what drew us together, especially if we have little in common except for the spark that was lit between us the instant we met.

If you're super intuitive, you might recognize the significance of this magnetic pull right away. But if you're a more intellectual type and you tend to analyze your thoughts before feeling your feelings, this realization can be shocking, overwhelming, and confusing at first. In some cases, realizing you've made a soul connection—whether you come to the understanding weeks, months, or years after that first bewildering meeting—can be a huge relief, because it makes sense of the emotional, physical, and spiritual intensity of the connection.

How to Use This Book

Conventional relationships and soul-based relationships often feel different when explored in depth—they face different challenges and offer different opportunities for healing and growth. In the chapters ahead, we'll dig into all the ways we can tease apart conventional romantic relationships from soulmate and Twin Flame relationships, and look at how we can grow and heal, even when things get complicated and past trauma is triggered. Starting at a foundational level—exploring different cultural beliefs about the soul—this book will provide you with the tools necessary to identify a Twin Flame relationship and navigate through every stage of this intense emotional, physical, and spiritual connection.

Throughout the book, I'll draw on different case studies to offer examples of the themes and concepts in action. You'll meet three pairs of Twin Flames, each one illustrating a different type of relationship, with a different trajectory. Each case study is a fictionalized amalgam of my client work, my research, and my own imagination—while the specifics are invented, the underlying emotions are very real and might feel familiar if you've been in a soul-to-soul partnership before. I'll sometimes refer to relationships that aren't soul-based as "conventional" partnerships, and when I speak about the partners in soul-based relationships, including ones that aren't specifically Twin Flames, I'll call them "soul familiars."

The book also includes a foldout poster which highlights different types of soul familiars. It can be used as an at-a-glance guide to help you differentiate and honor these deep spiritual connections and explore the lessons they bring with them into our lives.

* * *

1

THE SOUL ACROSS CULTURES

Whether we were raised in a religious or secular household, at some point in our lives we might meet a soul we've encountered before. Across cultures, faiths, and belief systems, most people, no matter what their background, retain an idea of the soul as an entity that exists. It's rare that we meet a person, even one with a strictly scientific mind, who claims that humans don't have souls. Even some atheists (those who don't believe in any god or divine being) say that they believe in the existence of the soul.

A Brief History of the Soul

From the ancient Sufis to Plato to modern New Age writers like Barbara Hand Clow and Elizabeth Clare Prophet, many have offered explanations not only for the concept of the soul, but for its journey through lifetimes and its encounters with other souls.

The word *soul* is derived from the Middle English *soule*, from the Old English *sawol*, and the Proto-Germanic *saiwalō*, and is defined by Merriam-Webster primarily as "the immaterial essence, animating principle, or actuating cause of an individual life." The ancient Greek word for soul is *psyche*, which also means "breath" or "life force," and the Latin name for soul is "anima," a term used by psychoanalyst Carl Jung, whose concepts we'll explore later in this book.

Nearly every culture and religion has a concept of the soul, including Judaism, Hinduism, Christianity, Islam, Buddhism, and beyond. If we try to distill the concept of the soul to its simplest, most essential meaning across cultures, it might not sound too far off from the definition listed above: *the non-corporeal essence or spirit of a living being, believed to live on after the person's death.* But the soul, for some people, is something inherently felt and understood that doesn't require an explanation. Some of us seem to arrive here on earth knowing what souls are.

If you believe that souls exist, you might also believe that your current lifetime is just that: current. By this, I mean that you live in a body now, but your soul has a past and a future which are not limited by time, space, dimensions, or death. Your body will eventually turn back to dust, but this is not your soul's first rodeo, and it likely will not be its last. The Hindus call this cycle of reincarnation samsara. Buddhists also use the term samsara to describe a cycle of reincarnation, and depict it visually using the motif of the wheel of life, or *Bhavacakra.*

Let's take a look at how a few different cultures and religions conceive of the soul.

The Buddhist Soul

Buddhism differs from many other faiths in that it adheres to a concept of "no soul" or anatta—but Buddhists do believe in a concept of rebirth. There is a continuity between incarnations that relies on karma, eventually leading to nirvana, or liberation from the cycle of birth and death.

The Christian Soul

Although there are many sects of Christianity with different beliefs, most branches of this monotheistic religion understand the soul as given to the body by God before birth. Upon the death of the body, the soul moves on to an afterlife that could be heaven or hell. (Catholics also believe in purgatory, a place where souls go to be purified through suffering before they can ascend to heaven.) There is no concept of reincarnation in Christianity.

The Hindu Soul

Hinduism, a religion founded on the Indian continent some 4,000 years ago, relies on the concept of Atman, the pure self or true nature of a person that goes beyond the body. Cycles of life and death are one of the main themes of Hindu belief systems, and this includes the idea that souls may reincarnate many times into many different bodies and eventually transcend the body entirely. The body is a mere costume for an eternal, unchanging soul that must collect good karma across lifetimes in order to transcend the cycle of reincarnation and achieve unity with Brahman, the ineffable ultimate reality of the universe.

The Abrahamic Faiths and the Twin Flame Journey

The Abrahamic faiths—Judaism, Christianity, and Islam—are monotheistic religions that trace their spiritual lineage to the patriarch Abraham, emphasizing a belief in one God, sacred texts, and moral teachings. These faiths share common roots, yet differ in practices, doctrines, and interpretations of divine revelation.

These faiths often present love and connection through frameworks of devotion, sacrifice, and divine will. Within these traditions, the concept of soul union and the transformative power of love is ever-present, albeit framed in ways that may seem at odds with the contemporary narrative of the Twin Flame journey. And yet, when we look closely, we see that these ancient teachings offer profound wisdom for those traversing the path of soul connection.

In Judaism, the notion of *basherte*—a destined partner—echoes the idea of a predestined soul connection that transcends mere coincidence. Rooted in the belief that all souls are interconnected and that certain people are meant to meet at pivotal moments, it parallels the Twin Flame experience, where union isn't just about romantic fulfillment but about spiritual awakening and growth. In the Kabbalistic teachings, the soul is said to split into two halves, male and female, which must ultimately reunite. This echoes the very essence of the Twin Flame connection: a soul fragmented by time and space, searching for its other half across lifetimes.

Christianity, too, touches on themes of divine union, though often in the context of the soul's relationship with Christ. The idea of a union between the soul and the divine can mirror the longing and intensity felt in the Twin Flame journey, where love is not just an earthly pursuit but a spiritual one, reflecting a return to the source. The concept of *agape*—divine, unconditional love—can be seen as a precursor to the transformative love that occurs when two souls, once separated, reunite in a moment of profound awakening.

In Islam, the concept of *ishq*—a passionate love for the divine—reminds us of the intensity of connection that exists between the lover and the beloved, a dynamic that can be reflected in the intensity and depth of a Twin Flame relationship. The Sufi tradition, with its focus on the yearning for the divine, offers a path of devotion that mirrors the inner transformation that occurs when one soul meets its counterpart. The path of ishq is not one of easy union but of spiritual surrender, of yearning and becoming—a journey that resonates with the challenges and revelations found on the Twin Flame path.

In all these traditions, love is not just a human experience but a sacred force that drives the soul toward reunion—with itself, with the divine, and with its counterpart on earth. The Abrahamic faiths, in their varied expressions, remind us that the journey of the soul is one of transformation, healing, and ultimately, union—both with others and with the divine. And while the language may differ, the underlying truth remains the same: Love, in all its forms, is the most powerful force in the universe.

The Jewish Soul

Judaism is another monotheistic religion (and an Abrahamic faith, like Islam and Christianity) whose concept of the soul (called *Neshama* in Hebrew) is complex and layered, with many soul "levels" that individuals move through. The soul is believed to be a person's God-given, eternal essence. In Kabbalah, the mystical branch of Judaism, there is a kind of reincarnation of the soul called *gilgul*, or *Gilgul Neshamot*. This is a concept of reincarnation or transmigration of souls, describing a cyclical journey of souls through multiple lifetimes, where they are reborn into different bodies to rectify mistakes and attempt to achieve spiritual perfection. The term "gilgul" itself means "cycle" or "wheel" in Hebrew.

The Muslim Soul

In Islam, a monotheistic religion that dates to the early 7th century and started in present-day Saudi Arabia, the soul is thought to be created by God (Allah) and breathed into the body before birth. The soul lives on after death, and its true nature is mysterious and only understood by Allah. There is an afterlife, but there is no reincarnation, so souls cannot "meet again" according to Muslim theology. (There are a few sects of Islam that do have a concept of reincarnation, such as certain Sufi traditions and the Druze.)

The Pagan Soul

Paganism covers a wide swath of beliefs, many based on pre-Christian and non-Abrahamic spiritual traditions that worship nature, including Norse, Celtic, Greek, Roman, and Egyptian traditions. Neo-pagans sometimes identify as Wiccans or witches. The soul in these traditions is often thought to exist before birth and after death, and can reincarnate, or remain on the earth plane as a spirit or ancestor.

The Secular Soul

Many secular people (those who don't adhere to any religion) still believe in the idea of the soul, and they may have a mishmash of different ideas about what their soul is and does. Often, people who don't believe in a divine being think of souls more in terms of their connections to other people, rather than about where the soul might go after death. In other words, the soul is a kind of divine doorway between beings; an expression of love and compassion; a light inside of us. The secular soul might also be understood as a metaphor or symbol for our consciousness or selfhood. This is particularly the case for secular humanists, who see souls as the moral core of a person, a source of dignity and compassion.

The Eclecticism of New Age Philosophy

New Age thinkers have always borrowed liberally from various religions, dating back to the movement's origins in the 19th century. The occultists, spiritualists, and theosophists of the time relied on concepts of the soul from Hinduism, Kabbalah, and Gnosticism, a belief system which emerged in the early centuries of the Common Era and draws from a blend of Hellenistic, Jewish, and Eastern mystical traditions.

The seeds of New Age philosophy were especially visible in the teachings of Helena Blavatsky, the Russian mystic and cofounder of the Theosophical Society in 1875. Drawing on Hindu metaphysics, Buddhist cosmology, and Western esotericism, Blavatsky helped lay the foundation for what would later become New Age cosmology: an evolving soul on a path toward higher consciousness, cycling through lifetimes, capable of psychic expansion and divine union. These ideas were radical for the Victorian era and appealed to seekers disillusioned with organized religion. But they were also shot through with the prejudices of their time: colonialist fascination with "Eastern wisdom," racial hierarchies masked as spiritual evolution, and uncritical elitism cloaked in mystical language.

Later on, many Westerners traveled to India in the 1960s and 1970s in search of spiritual guidance, and they brought back with them the concepts of karma and reincarnation (along with practices like yoga and meditation, the chakra system, and a broad concept of "spiritual transformation.") Alongside Eastern influences, the modern New Age movement also absorbed strands of Western mystical thought. Esoteric Christianity, Jungian psychology, alchemy, and astrology all contributed to its eclectic patchwork. By the 1980s, the movement had been commodified into self-help bestsellers, crystal catalogs, and meditation tapes promising higher love or instant karma.

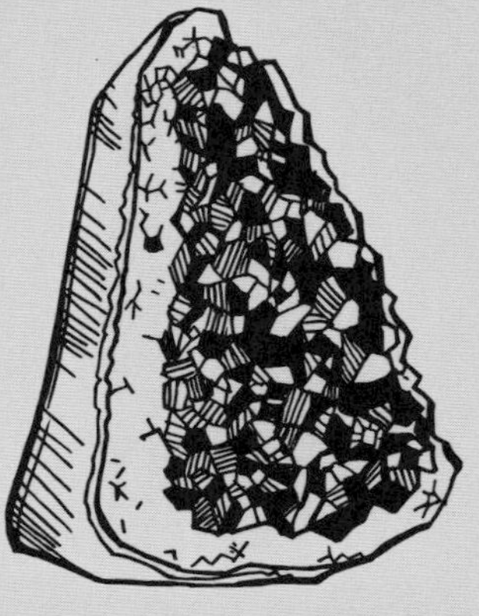

By the 1990s and 2000s, terms like "ascension," "soul contract," and "vibrational frequency" had become common parlance among New Age practitioners and influencers, but often without clarity or consensus about their meanings. The rise of social media platforms in the 2010s accelerated this phenomenon, enabling an explosion of Twin Flame content that could be deeply moving, but also dangerously simplistic. Claims of predestined reunion, spiritual hierarchy, or "runner/chaser" dynamics were increasingly marketed to vulnerable people navigating intense emotional pain, including those healing from trauma or abusive relationships. Some communities, such as "Twin Flames Universe," have been heavily criticized for exploiting that pain for financial gain or cult-like control. (Twin Flame Universe, in particular, is actually considered a cult and is the subject of a Netflix documentary. It's extremely controversial, and former members have come forward with claims of abuse.)

As we explore the concept of Twin Flames, it's important to acknowledge that a lot of New Age philosophy that came out of the late 20th century is indeed problematic, relying on sexist, heteronormative, white supremacist tropes, and rooted in commercialism. This has infected some of the discourse about Twin Flames, particularly around male-female pairings.

Acknowledging that the evolution and dissemination of New Age beliefs and practices began with a process of cultural extraction rooted in colonialism, racism, and sexism—and that many influential New Age thinkers were oblivious to the institutional systems that empowered them—is necessary. When we apply this lens, we are better able to filter through the outdated biases and assumptions informing some foundational New Age texts and reframe the most resonant concepts from this contemporary spiritual movement. Pursued with care, compassion, and inclusive language, we can dive deep into ideas like soul familiars and Twin Flames without causing more harm.

SARAH AND AMANI

In the suburbs of Chicago in the 1990s at a public elementary school, Sarah was a second grader from a Jewish family of Polish and Ukrainian descent, a third-generation American whose grandparents had survived the Holocaust. Amani was also in second grade, the first-generation daughter of Palestinian parents who had emigrated from Lebanon to the US in 1988. They weren't in the same class, but one day in the fall of 1994, Sarah saw Amani eating her lunch in the cafeteria and sat down next to her. She later said she just felt drawn to her, like she was a member of her own family. Sarah commented on the dates Amani was eating, because her mom often gave her dates as a sweet treat too. Amani smiled and offered Sarah a date, and they soon became best friends, eating lunch together every day and playing outside during recess.

Of course, they wanted to have playdates. Neither girl's parents expressed any concerns to their daughters directly, but both families worried privately that if talk of world events ever came up, it could be problematic for the girls. But this was right around the time a peace agreement was being negotiated between Israel and Palestine, and the families had hope, too.

On sleepovers, Amani and Sarah would talk deep into the night about their families and what they knew of their histories. Sarah shared the terrible stories she'd heard about the Holocaust. Amani had been a baby when her parents had brought her to the US, fleeing as war broke out all around them. She had some major trauma from these early childhood experiences, and she shared it all with Sarah—she'd never talked about it with anyone else.

The girls remained inseparable best friends all through elementary, junior high, and high school. They were like sisters, and would sometimes fight like sisters, but never about the politics that their parents assumed might separate them. They each had nightmares about what their ancestors had been through: This was their deepest bond.

Sarah had cousins in Tel Aviv and went to visit them for her bat mitzvah, and she returned to tell Amani every detail. Years after the war ended, Amani was able to go home and see family who had been left behind, and she returned with stories of their joyful reunion. It never occurred to either of them that geopolitics would get in the way of their close friendship. It was only when they both went away to college in 2001 that everything changed.

Part of the purpose of this book is to help us engage with New Age ideas and religious concepts more ethically—by tracing their origins, acknowledging their limitations, and choosing carefully which parts still resonate in a contemporary, inclusive, trauma-informed context. If Twin Flames exist, they do not require us to regress into binary gender roles or outdated ideas of soul hierarchies. They invite us to evolve into a more expansive, nuanced, and relational form of love.

* * *

2

SOUL FAMILIARS

We can certainly survive without primary romantic partnerships, and increasingly, many people choose to remain happily single. The sort of partnerships we crave may change throughout our lifetimes. But whether you want to be partnered or choose to fly solo, sometimes you meet someone who instantly turns your life upside down, and you have no map to help you navigate your connection with them. People whose lives are drastically altered by an intense relationship might eventually realize that their connection goes beyond the corporeal: They've known this soul before, and the relationship may not have been all unicorns and rainbows the first time around. There can be complicated karma to work out. And if you've met your Twin Flame, the two of you are instinctively trying to become whole again—which can be an excruciatingly painful process.

In some conventional romantic relationships, we may have initially found our partner attractive, funny, intriguing, dependable, intelligent, or simply easy to talk to. Maybe they reminded us of an ex, or a parent, or they fit our usual attachment pattern. Maybe we just needed somebody to keep us company during a lonely phase. Often our attraction to another person is thanks to a combination of the above. There are as many different reasons why people fall in love as there are people!

But when you meet someone with whom you share a soul connection, you often know something mysterious is up instantly, at least at the subconscious level. The hair on the back of your neck stands up. You get goose bumps. Your belly fills with butterflies. Your nervous system reacts to your activated subconscious mind. It's a feeling, an intuition. It's never easy to explain, even in retrospect.

When Soul Familiars Meet Again

Have you ever met someone in a class, at a party, or some other event and felt an instant sense of familiarity with them? Whether you're introduced by friends or randomly start talking while in line for the bathroom, you might feel an uncanny sensation telling you, "I already know this person." People meeting someone whose soul they recognize often think at first that they *literally* knew them in years past, asking, "Have we met?" Then follows a litany of possibilities: Did they live in the same town? Go to the same college? Work at the same company? Travel in the same circles?

No, no, no, and no. It becomes clear pretty quickly: You've never actually crossed paths in this lifetime. But your souls? They've definitely danced this dance before.

You might immediately become fast friends, having marathon conversations that feel breathless and deeply exhilarating, just because you "clicked" and want to know each other better. You might feel a mixture of attraction and revulsion

ALEX AND SIDNEY

Alex was a divorced mom of two kids in her early forties who worked in advertising and commuted to work in Manhattan each morning from New Jersey. One morning she slept through her alarm and woke up in a panic after a strange dream, missing her usual train to work. In the dream, she was walking barefoot on the pavement on the street outside her office, carrying her shoes in her hand. She walked right up to a very tall, handsome man in a forest green T-shirt, and began talking to him as if they were finishing a conversation they'd already started. Just before she woke up, she wondered, "Who is this man and why am I talking to him?"

Because she'd arrived late to work, she'd lined up afterschool childcare for her kids so she could stay an extra few hours at the office. As she was heading down the office corridor to her desk, she saw him and stopped dead in her tracks: The man from her dream was walking into a conference room with one of her colleagues. She felt the blood drain from her face and leaned against the wall.

Alex wasn't a terribly spiritual person, so this freaked her out considerably—she was absolutely certain that it was the very same man she'd dreamt about mere hours earlier. She watched through the glass as he sat down with her colleague Greg and then tried to gather herself to make it back to her desk.

Before she could step away, it happened: Greg spotted her standing there and waved her into the conference room. Later, she couldn't remember what she was thinking or feeling as she crossed the room to the two men, but when Sidney was introduced and she shook his extended hand, it was like touching a live wire; she was sure that she visibly jumped.

Sid felt the same wild spark. He was a handsome man in his late twenties, from a completely different world than Alex: younger, single, without kids, living a high-speed life in the city rather than settling down in the suburbs. He was a friend of her colleague Greg, who was hiring Sidney for a freelance design project. Sid would be reporting directly to Alex.

It would be months before Alex told Sid about her dream, but their work relationship quickly turned intensely romantic and sexual, even though Sid was in a long-term relationship—one that he had thought he was happy in.

right away, asking yourself: Why can't I stop thinking about this person, even though they're clearly not right for me?

Alternatively, you might run into them randomly again and again. Perhaps the initial meeting didn't strike you as very meaningful, but now that you've seen them in the supermarket, the post office, and picking up their kid at school, you're wondering why these encounters have become a pattern in your life. When the universe is really trying to get your attention, you might have a dream about a soul familiar before meeting them in the flesh.

Most soul familiars feel *something* profound when they meet each other. I'll dive deeper into our nervous system response in Chapter Three, but it's important to note: No matter what the relationship turns out to be for us—whether we've met a soulmate, a karmic partner, or a Twin Flame—if we're paying attention to our intuition, there's usually a sign right at the start.

Understanding Soulmates

Soulmates are the subject of movies, novels, and regular conversation. You've surely heard a friend declare, "I think I've met my soulmate!" after meeting someone they're falling in love with. Yet they may end up in a conventional love relationship, where their connection is based on shared values, attraction, and empathy.

"Soulmate"

According to the Oxford English Dictionary, the first known use of the term "soulmate" was in a letter from poet and philosopher Samuel Taylor Coleridge in 1822. He said, "to be happy in married life, you must have a soul-mate." But as we're learning in this book, the bond between soul familiars can take many shapes beyond conventional marriage.

Of all the possible configurations of soul familiars, soulmates are probably the best known, and the easiest to understand. A soulmate could be anyone with whom you share a deep bond, one that feels like it might transcend your current lifetime.

Plato proposed a soulmate theory in his *Symposium*: He suggested that soulmates were once one body, split in two by a jealous Zeus. (This may actually be one of the myths that influenced the Twin Flame concept.) But Plato wasn't talking about what we feel when we actually meet a soulmate: He was talking about why we might *long* for one, which is another matter entirely.

Our modern understanding of what a soulmate is varies, but the most common definition is a relationship that feels essential, ordained, or meant to be. We might call our soulmate our "ride or die," someone we'll always be there for us (and vice versa). But even this understanding misses a core truth: Why did we choose this particular person? How does our soul recognize their soul?

To call someone a soulmate typically suggests, in addition to the "meant to be" quality of the relationship, that your bond with one another is positive. Soulmates tend to make us feel enriched and help us blossom, rather than bringing out a shadow side of the personality, as often happens with Twin Flames. When we find a soulmate, whether they're a romantic partner, a deep friend, or a member of our family with whom we're particularly close, we feel seen and understood. These relationships tend to inspire less jealousy than Twin Flame relationships do.

When we spend time apart from a soulmate, for example, we might miss them, but without the fear that that separation will harm us. In a healthy soulmate relationship, if all other conditions are right, we might experience something the polyamorous community calls "compersion," which loosely translates into, "I feel pleasure when my partner feels pleasure." A true soulmate loves you and honors your needs, your personal space, and even your autonomy, because deep down, they know you've been together before and you will be again. They are not threatened when you don't need them.

With both karmic relationships and Twin Flames, there is more of a sense of unfinished business, the kind that was left unresolved in a prior lifetime, leaving one or both partners in a state of trauma or grief. With soulmates, it might feel like the healing already took place, so when you reunite in this lifetime, you're ready to support and love one another.

Understanding Karmic Relationships

Karmic relationships also inspire that instant familiarity, a sense that you've known each other before. But unlike when soulmates meet, when you encounter someone with whom you share a karmic relationship, you're more likely to be triggered both intensely and instantly. In these relationships, lessons are learned quickly.

Karma is an ancient Indian concept that essentially says that all actions have consequences that play out across the different lifetimes of our souls. According to Hindu scripture, karma can be broken down into four categories (more detail to follow), and it's often associated with rebirth/reincarnation. It's worth noting, however, that different schools of Hinduism interpret the concept in different ways.

The New Age concept of karma is loosely based on the idea that there is cause and effect in the universe. But how does all of this apply to karmic *relationships*? When we are bound in a karmic relationship with someone, it's often the case that they wronged or hurt us in a previous life—or that we wronged or hurt them. When we meet again, we might feel emotionally activated in ways that are seemingly out of proportion to their actions. For example, a karmic relationship could look like getting into a fender bender with someone with whom you argued in a previous lifetime. Maybe your first

The Four Categories of Hindu Karma

Karma is one of the most misunderstood concepts in spiritual discourse—often flattened into a pop-culture punchline about revenge or divine justice. But in the Hindu traditions from which the idea originates, karma is not about blame or punishment; it's about continuity. Karma is the energetic residue left by an incarnated soul's actions—not just their physical deeds, but also their words, thoughts, and intentions. We might understand karma in this context as the soul's memory of its own becoming. And in many Hindu philosophical schools, karma is categorized into four types, each describing a different phase in this ongoing process.

Sanchita karma is the total karmic accumulation of all your past lives. Every embodied lifetime leaves an imprint, and those impressions are stored in the soul—like files in an infinite archive. This is your karmic inheritance—not in a linear or punitive sense, but in a subtler way: a spiritual reservoir of unprocessed material, unfulfilled intentions, and unresolved patterns. It's not all destined to manifest in one lifetime, but it's always there in the background, shaping our potential.

Prarabdha karma is the sliver of that archive currently unfolding in this life. It's the karma that has ripened—the reason you were born into a specific family, body, geography, or socioeconomic context. These are the cards you're playing with in this incarnation. You don't get to choose them consciously, but you do have the agency to respond. That response determines whether you perpetuate the karmic cycle or begin to shift it.

Kriyamana karma is what you're creating now. This is the karma generated by your current actions, thoughts, and emotional responses—the part you have the most direct influence over. Every conscious decision, every moment of compassion or cruelty, adds to this thread. This is where self-awareness becomes the most powerful spiritual tool: The more awake you are to your motivations, the more you can steer your soul's evolution.

Agami karma refers to the karma being generated now that will bear fruit in future lives. It's the forward-looking echo of your current intentions—the energetic signature of your choices that will shape what comes next.

Together, these four types of karma describe a soul in motion: gathering, unfolding, creating, and projecting. They invite us into a relationship with time that is both vast and intimate, where nothing is ever wasted—and everything can be transformed.

instinct is to feel rage because your car is dinged, but you exchange information and the insurance company covers it; no harm, no foul. Next time around, you and this other soul don't need to meet again.

Say you encounter a karmic soul familiar in a bar, while out with friends. You might be instantly attracted to them, but also feel like there's some major red flag that you can't immediately identify. But still, you're compelled to go out with them when they ask. On your first date, you realize that your politics are staunchly opposed and you argue, and yet, for some reason, you still feel compelled to sleep with them. The entire relationship lasts just three weeks, plagued by constant bickering. In the end, you block each other on all social media platforms. The whirlwind of it all leaves you exhausted and having learned a profound lesson: You need to be around people who share your most closely held values and worldview.

This sort of encounter displays all the hallmarks of a karmic relationship. The hint came at the beginning in the initial attraction that felt almost like an instinctual pull. Perhaps your souls knew each other before, and saw the world in very different ways, but were forced to spend time together. Maybe you were in an arranged marriage, or worked as a boss and employee, or were somehow pushed together despite coming from very different belief systems. The lesson you learn from a karmic relationship is often tied to precisely why you were in each other's lives last time around.

Even though the volatility, toxicity, and tumultuousness of karmic relationships can feel similar to a Twin Flame relationship, they have two key differences: First, a karmic relationship is typically quick and dirty, while a Twin Flame relationship can last a lifetime. Karmic relationships typically aren't resolvable, or at least not resolvable in ways that allow for a successful romantic relationship. Rarely, people in karmic relationships can remain friends or acquaintances, but often this isn't necessary or desired after the lessons have been learned. The other key difference is that karmic relationships are thought to be an encounter of two separate souls, whereas Twin Flames are the separated halves of a single soul. This is why it takes so much psychological digging to eventually heal and reintegrate after a Twin Flame relationship begins.

Understanding Twin Flames

Of all the types of soul familiars we can encounter, Twin Flames are the most complex, layered, and life-changing. These relationships often seem impossible to understand, and it can take years to tease them apart and heal from them. On the ever-winding path of love and self-evolution, Twin Flame relationships remain alluring, elusive, and often misunderstood. Twin Flame relationships are not just another love story. They are the *mirror* that forces you to see your soul in its most raw and radiant form.

Unlike most soulmate encounters, meeting a Twin Flame can feel like being struck by lightning. These relationships tend to shake you up and awaken you to new parts of yourself.

A Twin Flame is thought to be the *other half of your soul*, split from the same energetic source long before this current lifetime began. You and your Twin Flame may have agreed, somewhere along the wheel of time, to find each other next time around. You're not necessarily seeking to complete each other, but to ignite a transformation that could only happen through this bond. When you meet them, a part of you will recognize them immediately, even if you've never met before in this life. The recognition may be totally subconscious, but the biggest tell of all is how your nervous system responds to seeing them the first time (more on this in Chapter Three).

The Mirror Effect

Your Twin Flame reflects your deepest wounds, your unconscious patterns, and your buried desires. You see yourself fully in their eyes, which is simultaneously seductive and terrifying. Twin Flames won't let you hide; they show up to burn away your own illusions. They certainly don't know they're doing this, and you probably won't know consciously at first—but in that first meeting, even in the first few seconds, the soul knows.

This is why many Twin Flame relationships involve separation, conflict, and even long stretches of silence. It's not because the love isn't real; it's because the healing is so necessary and raw that it can feel like nothing else you've ever experienced.

One of the most well-known patterns of a Twin Flame journey is the runner-chaser dynamic. One person often pulls away (the runner), overwhelmed by the intensity of the connection, while the other feels abandoned (the chaser), trying to maintain the closeness. But underneath this painful pattern is a deeper truth: Both are avoiding parts of themselves. The runner fears being seen; the chaser fears being alone. The universe won't let you come back together fully until you've both done the soul work.

Identifying a Soul Connection

Twin Flames, soulmates, and karmic relationships each arrive in your life like different seasons. They're all transformative, but with distinct emotional textures.

Soulmates are your sacred soft places to land—people you've journeyed with before in other lifetimes who feel like home the moment you meet them. They support your growth gently, with warmth and mutual understanding. Soulmates don't necessarily stir chaos; they offer comfort, resonance, and a sense of "I've known you forever." These relationships can be romantic, platonic, or familial, and they don't demand drama to be deeply meaningful.

Karmic relationships, by contrast, are cosmic teachers that don't knock—they barge in. These unions are heavy with emotional contracts, often filled with sudden rage, intense attraction, and important lessons. They feel urgent and consuming but are usually temporary.

What Is Past Life Regression?

Past life regression is a therapeutic and spiritual practice rooted in the belief that our souls carry imprints from previous incarnations. Through guided hypnosis, deep meditation, or altered states of consciousness, a practitioner helps an individual access memories or impressions believed to be from another lifetime. These glimpses are often emotional, sensory, or symbolic rather than linear, and may illuminate persistent patterns, fears, longings, or unresolved relational dynamics.

The idea of reincarnation is ancient, but Western interest in past lives surged in the mid-20th century within the New Age movement, which blends Eastern cosmologies with Western psychotherapy. Pioneers like Dr. Brian Weiss popularized the practice of past life regression in the 1980s, framing it as a form of healing. His work suggested that understanding a soul's karmic history could release emotional blockages or clarify the deeper roots of a phobia, chronic illness, or intense relationship.

While powerful, past life regression can be highly subjective. Some experience these regressions as vivid narratives; others receive more impressionistic flashes, including colors, sensations, or inexplicable emotional responses tied to particular time periods or places. Practitioners often encourage clients not to force coherence or logic onto what arises. What emerges in a session may be metaphor, memory, or something else entirely, but that doesn't make it meaningless. Like dreams, these inner journeys speak in the language of the unconscious.

Whether literal or symbolic, what's revealed can catalyze deep shifts: grief that finally surfaces, phobias that resolve, or persistent relational dynamics that begin to make emotional sense in a larger arc of meaning.

It's important to approach this practice with discernment. Not all who offer regression work are trauma-informed, and not all experiences are healing. But when held in a safe, ethical, and grounded container, past life regression can offer a way to reconnect to the soul's journey—and begin to release what no longer serves. For people in Twin Flame relationships, this is essential.

What Are the Akashic Records?

The Akashic Records are often described as an energetic archive of every soul's journey—past, present, and potential. Rooted in the Sanskrit word *ākāśa*, meaning ether or sky, the Akashic field is said to hold a vibrational imprint of all thoughts, emotions, choices, and experiences across time. In this view, everything that has ever occurred–and every path a soul might take—is encoded in this subtle, non-physical plane of consciousness. Think of it like a cosmic library.

Although the concept has deep linguistic and metaphysical roots in Eastern philosophy, what most contemporary seekers refer to as the Akashic Records emerged from a 19th-century Western esoteric context. Theosophists like Helena Blavatsky and Charles Leadbeater popularized the idea in the late 1800s, blending Eastern cosmology, Christian mysticism, and occult practices.

In the New Age era, the Akashic Records became widely known as a source of spiritual information which intuitive readers could "enter" through meditation, prayer, or channeling techniques. Today, many practitioners use Akashic Record readings to help individuals understand repeating patterns, karmic connections, soul contracts, or life lessons that may be influencing their current path—especially in profound spiritual relationships, like those framed as Twin Flames.

As with past life regression, Akashic Record readings operate in a liminal space between symbolism and belief. The content that emerges in a session might not be "true" in a factual, historical sense—but that doesn't negate its emotional or psychological resonance. The soul may speak in images, archetypes, or metaphor. When approached with discernment, a reading can offer insight into what feels stuck or mysterious in a person's life, providing clarity, comfort, or validation.

Still, the Akashic Records are not a substitute for self-inquiry, relational accountability, or therapeutic work. Accessing this space is not about spiritual escapism or outsourcing our choices to cosmic authority. Instead, it's an invitation to delve more deeply into the story our soul is telling—especially important if we're trying to understand the ways in which a Twin Flame partner has rocked our entire world.

Twin Flames, though, are in a class of their own. They force you to face your shadows, to burn away your ego, and to rise as your most authentic self. Unlike karmic relationships, Twin Flames aren't about clearing karma, debt, or punishment. The lesson isn't to hold on to each other, but to each evolve into a higher version of themselves—whether they end up together or not.

At the very beginning, Twin Flame relationships and karmic relationships can feel somatically and emotionally identical. If you're in a relationship right now and you already know that your partner is a soul familiar but can't quite tease out whether you're with a soulmate, a karmic familiar, or a Twin Flame, that's okay. Often, especially in the case of Twin Flames, it takes some time to suss out the origin of your connection. You may not ever be totally sure, in spite of having a strong feeling or instinct about it. You might ask your partner to talk it through with you, to offer confirmation or insight from their perspective. You might also do a past life regression or Akashic Records reading together.

But if they won't do the research with you, or they think the concept is hokey—or if you're not ready to share your suspicion with them—you can still work through this topic on your own and see what resonates with you.

Other Kinds of Soul Familiars

In addition to the familiar concepts of soulmates, Twin Flames, and karmic relationships, there are other ways to understand the souls that meet again across lifetimes. Consider the concept of "soul groups." These are collections of souls that have traveled together through multiple incarnations, playing different roles with one another in each life, yet always connected by a deeper, overarching bond. In each lifetime, members of a soul group may come together to challenge, support, and guide one another, but the connection remains constant, no matter the specific form it takes.

This bond transcends the individual experience, creating a sense of shared history and purpose, across time. Soul groups can take the shape of families, groups of friends, or even polycules. (A polycule is a web of interconnected, consensual relationships, where love and connection flow freely between individuals who are bound by the shared understanding and fluidity of their emotional and sexual bonds.)

Then there are companion souls, who share a special, often nurturing connection with one another. While these bonds are not always romantic, they can be just as profound. Companion souls show up for us in times of need, offering unconditional support and guidance, and playing a vital role in our

emotional and spiritual growth. The relationship may evolve in different ways over multiple lifetimes, but the essence of their connection remains anchored in the deep care and understanding they provide each other with.

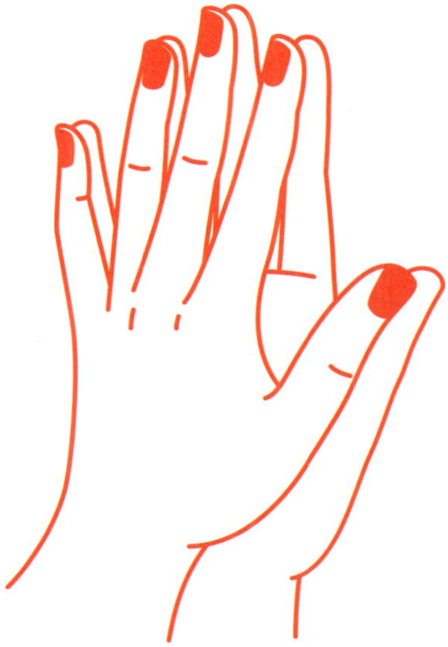

Mirror souls, while similar to Twin Flames, reflect one another's strengths, weaknesses, and unresolved shadows. Their connection may not be as intense as the Twin Flame bond, but it is no less significant. Mirror souls present us with an opportunity for growth by showing us the parts of ourselves that need healing or development. The relationship often holds a powerful mirror to the inner self, allowing us to confront and embrace our own contradictions.

Finally, past life lovers are souls that have shared a romantic connection in previous lifetimes. These souls are often drawn together again in new incarnations, either to rekindle a deep connection or to resolve issues left unresolved from their past together. The pull between past life lovers can feel magnetic, as though the bond is timeless and unbreakable, yet always tied to the lessons of the past.

These varied categories of soul familiars emphasize the deep, intricate web of relationships that weave through multiple lifetimes. Each bond—whether it be from a soul group, as a companion, or through karmic entanglements—offers a unique opportunity for growth, healing, and ultimately, reunion both with the self and other.

* * *

3

THE BODY AND MIND RESPONSE

The hormones that flood our bodies in the honeymoon stage of a romantic or sexual relationship can feel just like the fight-or-flight sensations released into our body when two souls recognize each other. This isn't because we consciously perceive our potential partner as a threat: It's more that we are activated, and our nervous system understands that *this is a big deal.* In those first seconds, our nervous systems can often identify a soul familiar, long before our minds understand what has happened. You can feel it in your body, even if you don't immediately recognize the sensation. If you are inexplicably drawn to another person with whom you share no cultural ties or interests—even someone that you wouldn't ordinary find attractive—it might be that your souls are linked.

Understanding the Nervous System

Let's start with the basics. The nervous system is a brilliant part of our body that works in the background, controlling our digestion, our breathing, and our response to stimuli: all the things we're not consciously thinking about.

Your nervous system is the invisible architecture that governs everything from your heartbeat to your first kiss. It's the ultimate interface between your body, your environment, and your emotions. The nervous system is constantly scanning, reacting, soothing, and stimulating. If your body is the temple, your nervous system is the sacred circuitry that lights it up.

At its core, the nervous system has two main branches: the central nervous system (CNS) and the peripheral nervous system (PNS). But for our purposes—since we want to understand emotions, relationships, and self-regulation—we're going to focus on two important parts of the *peripheral* branch: the somatic and autonomic nervous systems.

The Somatic Nervous System

The somatic nervous system is your body's direct line to the outside world. It's responsible for all voluntary movements, like reaching out to touch a lover's hand, blinking when you get something in your eye, or dancing when your favorite song comes on. It sends sensory information to your brain and carries back the motor instructions that make your body move. It's conscious and deliberate. It's you *doing the thing*. But the deeper magic happens just beneath the surface.

The Autonomic Nervous System

The autonomic nervous system is like a behind-the-scenes director. It runs the show without you even noticing, regulating your heartbeat, digestion, breathing, and more. You don't have to *think* about speeding up your pulse when you're scared or calming down after a safe hug. Your body just *knows*.
This system has traditionally been divided into two branches:

- ★ **Sympathetic nervous system:** Think *go mode*. It's your fight-or-flight response, full of adrenaline and mobilization. It activates when you're in danger or need to hustle. This is the leftover part of human circuitry from the time when our ancestors might have encountered lions or other predators and would have needed to run for their lives. This is also what often ratchets up when we encounter a Twin Flame for the first time.
- ★ **Parasympathetic nervous system:** Think *rest and digest*. It's the calm after the storm; the softness that helps you slow down, breathe deeply, and feel safe.

First Date Jitters or Twin Flame Recognition?

As I mentioned earlier, sometimes our nervous system acts up even when we encounter someone who is *not* a Twin Flame or soul familiar, so it can be hard to know the difference. The truth is, you're likelier to understand this in retrospect—perhaps weeks, months, or even years after you've established the Twin Flame bond you share with someone.

Everyday dating anxiety can trigger the same parts of your nervous system that soul encounters can, and unfortunately your nervous system can't call you up to explain the difference.

Polyvagal Theory

Developed by Dr. Stephen Porges, polyvagal theory is like the love language of your nervous system. It says: We aren't just toggling between fight-or-flight and rest and digest. There's a third state, and it's all about connection. Using this theory, we can learn to "co-regulate" with our partner, finding peace and comfort instead of fear and rage.

The vagus nerve, a long, wandering nerve that connects your brain to your body, is the star of this show. It's the main player in the parasympathetic nervous system, but not all vagus nerve activity is the same. According to polyvagal theory, there are three states your nervous system can flow through:

1. **Ventral Vagal (Safety and Social Engagement)**
   This is your nervous system's version of a cozy fireside chat. You feel calm, grounded, and ready to connect. Eye contact, empathy, laughter, and intimacy all happen here. When your body senses safety, it invites you into this openhearted state. This is where we ideally want to be with a romantic partner or friend.

2. **Sympathetic (Mobilization/Fight-or-Flight)**
   When danger shows up, your body kicks into high gear. Your muscles tense and your heart races. You're not thinking about

bonding in this state: You're ready to run or defend yourself. This is essential when needed, but exhausting if it's chronic. It's a state that's commonly triggered in Twin Flame unions that have not yet been healed or resolved.

3. **Dorsal Vagal (Shutdown or Freeze)**
   This is the underworld of your nervous system: the state of collapse, disconnection, and numbness. It's what happens when fight-or-flight isn't possible. Think dissociation, withdrawal, or the "I'm fine" mask that hides real pain. It's your system protecting you through stillness. If you're in a state of grief after a Twin Flame relationship has ended, you might find yourself here.

Listening to Your Body's Wisdom

What polyvagal theory teaches us is that your nervous system isn't malfunctioning when you're in any of these states. It's doing exactly what it was designed to do: keep you safe. The more we learn to *notice* these states without judgment, the more we can gently guide ourselves back to connection. Through practices like breathwork, touch, eye contact, somatic therapy, or just slowing down, we can tend to our vagus nerve like a sacred thread weaving us back into a relationship with ourselves and others.

Even in a state of activation, you are not broken. You're brilliantly wired so that when you meet someone who lights up your nervous system, your body communicates with you in a primal, poetic language. When you honor your nervous system and give yourself permission to come home to safety, softness, and sacred connection, you can also heal your relationships.

But there are a few signs you can look for. First, the feeling that you've known the person before—that they're instantly recognizable to you—is much more common when you're meeting a soul familiar. You might feel shaky and wonder, "What am I getting myself into?" around a Twin Flame. Pay attention to sensation around the heart chakra, too. Different than merely a racing heart, which can happen in any conventional dating situation, with a Twin Flame, it might feel as though you're more *aware* of your heart, like it's trying to get your attention. The phrase "my heart swelled" might come to mind. You might also feel strangely weepy, especially when they say something that moves you, or if you feel like they're listening to you deeply. The sense of being truly seen can be alarming at first, especially if you're not used to it, and it activates the nervous system. This weepiness can also come up the first time you're physically intimate with a Twin Flame. I'll explore that combination of ecstasy and emotion in the next chapter.

Prolonged Hypervigilance

Our nervous system offers some additional clues to help diagnose a Twin Flame relationship. In a healthy conventional romantic relationship, even if you really like someone and are falling in love with them, after a reasonable period of time—sometimes weeks, occasionally months—those initial butterflies should transform into a sense of safety.

What Is Your Nervous System Telling You?

When we meet our soulmate or Twin Flame, our body usually tries to tell us in the first few seconds. Our subconscious mind may instantly recognize this lost but familiar soul, and although the prefrontal cortex of our brain can't quite compute it, our amygdala (the part of our brain that controls our fight-or-flight mechanism) lights up and sends a swirl of messages to different regions of our body. Common nervous system reactions upon encountering a familiar soul are:

- Sweaty palms, brow, and underarms; an overall feeling of heat rising through your body
- Shaky hands; a sensation of quaking, as if your whole body is speeding up
- Rapid heartbeat
- Stomach issues or "butterflies" (You might also suddenly feel like you have to poop.)
- Chills (This is what we might call "spine-tingling.")
- The inability to speak coherently because of all of this nervous system anxiety
- Uncontrollable blushing

What Is the Chakra System?

The chakra system is a map of the subtle body (the spiritual part of the body) that originated in ancient Indian spiritual and medical traditions. It was first described in early texts like the *Upanishads* and developed later in the *Yoga Sutras* and Tantric writings. This is one of the concepts that Westerners brought back with them after their spiritual journeys to India in the middle and late 20th century. Chakras are understood as energy centers that run along the spine, from the base of the pelvis to the crown of the head. Though interpretations vary, most modern descriptions name seven main chakras, each associated with a specific location in the body, as well as emotional themes and states of consciousness.

In contemporary Western spirituality, the chakras are often reduced to a pastel rainbow of affirmations, but their original meaning was far more complex. These energy centers weren't just seen as spinning disks of light, but as multidimensional loci of physical, emotional, spiritual, and karmic information. For example, the root chakra (*Muladhara*), located at the base of the spine, governs safety, survival, and material belonging; the heart chakra (*Anahata*) is tied to love, grief, and compassion; and the crown chakra (*Sahasrara*) is thought to connect us to divine consciousness or source. When we meet and engage with our Twin Flame partner, working with the chakras can be a useful tool, paying special attention to the heart chakra.

While Western frameworks can be powerful tools for healing and self-awareness, it's crucial to remember that they are filtered through layers of cultural interpretation and appropriation. Approaching the chakra system with reverence for its roots while also integrating it with therapeutic modalities like somatic work, trauma recovery, and shadow integration allows us to use it not just as a metaphor for energetic balance, but as a lens through which to understand our bodies, our longings, and our capacity for transformation.

But in a Twin Flame relationship, we might feel those butterflies for months or even years, especially if we haven't fully explored, understood, and healed from the past life trauma we're bringing to the relationship. We remain in a state of hypervigilance, where our nervous system is always "up," expecting the other shoe to drop. This can be incredibly challenging and confusing. In fact, it's similar to how people tend to feel in abusive relationships—you're going through each interaction with your partner expecting the ground to fall away beneath your feet with no warning and no way to get to safety. Your nervous system is working overtime.

* * *

4

SEX AND PASSION

When Twin Flame relationships are romantic, the sexual connection is often the first hint: It's powerful, highly charged, and often an instant draw. There are legendary stories from Twin Flame partners about the first time they saw each other, but the first time they touched each other? That's a whole different level of intensity.

We know from the previous chapter that our bodies, specifically our nervous system, can be excellent indicators when we're encountering a soul familiar. But physical intimacy reveals so much more. People describe the first time they were touched by their Twin Flame lover as akin to electricity running through their entire body, or seeing sparks shoot out of their lover's fingertips. Twin Flame lovers have described their first kiss with language like, "I saw a blinding white light," and, "I felt like I was floating."

And that's just kissing. When physical intimacy advances, and it often does so very quickly in Twin Flame relationships, lovers frequently describe their first time together as mind-blowing, ecstatic, addictive, and the best sex they've ever had. Whether or not they're religious or believe in any kind of God, there is a lot of divine language involved in descriptions of Twin Flame sex. It's the kind of sexual union that, even many years later, the partners can recall in exquisite detail. This is shooting-stars sex, sacred sex, sex that feels astonishingly pleasurable—it's often deeply spiritual and animalistic at the same time.

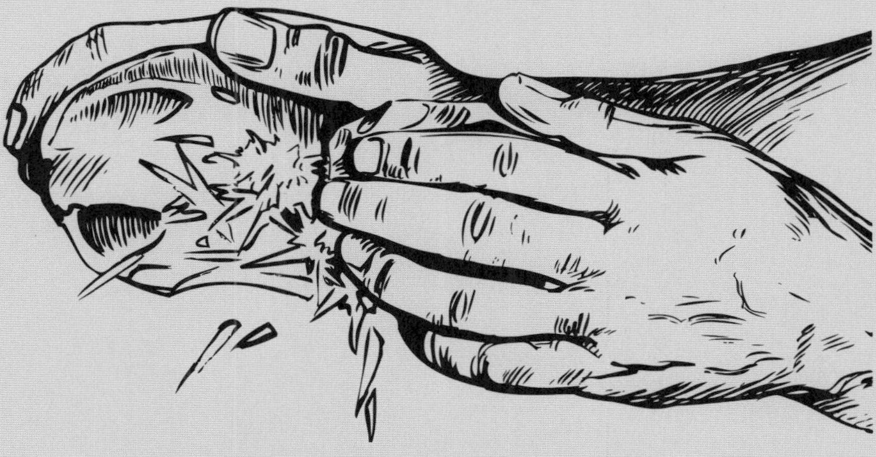

Often, when conventional partners describe the first time they had sex, one partner remembers it one way and the other remembers it another way, even when both remember it fondly. But for Twin Flames, both partners often report the same sensations and spiritual awakenings, along the same timeline. "Electricity" is a word that comes up again and again in descriptions of intimate encounters between Twin Flame lovers, and not just the first time—but almost every sexual encounter they have.

Think of it like this: When you're physically intimate with a Twin Flame lover, you're actually experiencing the most profound kind of intimacy—a soul-deep union with yourself. If we believe that a Twin Flame is a lost part of our own soul, then it makes sense that a carnal union might cause the separated souls to remember that they belong together.

It's very normal and common for sexual partners to experience orgasms at different times. For heterosexual couples, this is the rule, not the exception. "Coming together" is more of a rom-com fantasy than it is a reality for men and women who sleep together. In fact, a phenomenon called the "orgasm gap" describes how often women do not orgasm *at all* with their male partners. But if you're in a Twin Flame relationship, the elusive simultaneous orgasm is far more common, and it could be an indicator that your partner is indeed your Twin Flame.

NICK AND CLAIRE

Sometimes a meeting of Twin Flames is mundane, but sometimes it's a meet-cute straight out of a Hallmark rom-com. So it was for Nick and Claire, two busy New Yorkers on their way to work on a typical Tuesday morning. As Claire made her way to the Union Square train station, reading an email from her boss on her phone, she smacked directly into Nick, who had just stepped out of the coffee shop and was securing the cover of his latte.

BOOM. She was walking so fast he later joked that she had intentionally body-slammed him. The coffee fell to the floor, splashing all over Nick's coat. Claire was mortified and offered to pay for his dry cleaning. They exchanged numbers and went on their way. And after taking about ten steps, both of them stopped and looked back at each other.

Claire felt so dizzy after she stepped onto the R train that she needed to ask someone if she could take their seat. Meanwhile, Nick was sitting at his desk and furiously googling Claire. Within an hour, he had texted to invite her to dinner that night. She said yes.

They spent the day equally elated and terrified. Claire left work early so she could get ready for their date. When she got to the restaurant, Nick was waiting outside. Both of their hearts were beating furiously, and they hugged. Without warning, Claire began to tear up. She already knew this would be no ordinary relationship; she could feel it in her body.

Nick didn't understand his feelings. Up until he met Claire, he'd been dating in an unserious way, just having fun. But he was already imagining their second, third, and fourth date, and worrying about what she'd think of his apartment.

They laughed uproariously through dinner, and soon enough Claire did see the inside of Nick's apartment. She saw it again the next night, and the next. For both of them, this whirlwind romance was characterized by the best sex of their lives. Their repeated simultaneous orgasms shocked and delighted them, as they'd never experienced this with previous partners. The highs were extraordinarily high. Until one night three weeks in, when they spent a rare night apart. They went out separately with friends and unexpectedly ended up at the same bar. Nick was with a buddy from work and barely acknowledged Claire. She was enraged, stormed out the bar, cried hysterically, and decided it was over. But it was far from over. The drama was just beginning.

Unrequited Lust

Sometimes people will fall hard into a lust-fueled infatuation with someone, and in trying to figure out their intense and overwhelming feelings, mistakenly assume the object of their desire is a soul familiar. That can become a very unhealthy situation if it's not worked through, or if the one doing the lusting persists in believing that the subject of their lust is a soulmate or Twin Flame. If you're navigating something like that, hopefully this book can help you tease apart feelings of lust from a true past life connection.

This type of confusion can occur when someone is profoundly attracted to another person, but that attraction isn't reciprocated or the second person is not available. Perhaps they're already in a relationship which they're not ready to leave. Or sometimes, after a brief but heady affair ends, one partner can't stop thinking and fantasizing about the person they were with, even if they were only together for one night. Their friends and family might call them obsessed.

In situations like this, the feelings can be so profound and the desire so consuming that the person lusting will decide their partner must have been a Twin Flame. Otherwise, they tell themselves, why would they feel so much? It's important to understand that unrequited love, lust, and obsession are not at all uncommon, and the feelings stirred up by a brief tryst or even by a parasocial relationship with a celebrity can make us feel like we're special and unique, convinced that there must be some deep spiritual reason why we can't stop thinking about the object of our desire.

There are myriad reasons for people to fall into an infatuation that feels totally overwhelming and consuming, including past heartbreak, sexual shame, unhealed parental trauma, and unhealthy attachment styles. Working through these possibilities is a healthy step to take before you get lost in an internet deep dive and convince yourself that the person you desire is your Twin Flame and they just don't know it yet.

Navigating Lust and Sexual Obsession

Navigating obsessive sexual infatuations, sexual compulsivity, and the aftermath of intense encounters is a journey that demands deep self-awareness, emotional honesty, and the willingness to confront the parts of ourselves we might otherwise avoid—and this journey can be initiated or intensified by a Twin Flame encounter or relationship. When we find ourselves in the grip of an obsessive connection, especially one that burns with an intensity that feels impossible to resist, it can be difficult to discern where we end and the other begins. The line between love, lust, and obsession can blur, and in that blurring, we risk losing ourselves in a cycle of emotional highs and lows, chasing the high of infatuation, only to be pulled into the depths of disillusionment when the connection falters.

For those who find themselves caught in this cycle, the first step is understanding that what feels like a profound bond and physical connection may actually be rooted in a deeper need for validation, control, or escape. Often, obsessive infatuation stems from unhealed wounds within us—the desire to merge with someone else, to fill a void, or to find in another the parts of ourselves we have not yet fully embraced. In these moments, it's crucial to differentiate between love that is rooted in authentic connection and love that is driven by an unconscious attempt to heal wounds through external means. Cultivating a healthy relationship with your desire and cutting through sexual shame are a major part of this process.

One tool to begin this process is **mindfulness**. Mindfulness helps us to sit with the emotions that arise without immediately acting on them. In the context of sexual obsession, mindfulness allows us to observe the intensity of our feelings, without becoming consumed by them. It is not about repressing

desire or the impulse to merge with another; instead, it is about allowing ourselves the space to feel and to question, and to ask ourselves: What is it I truly want from this connection? Is this desire rooted in love, or is it a reaction to an unmet need within myself?

Part of the challenge with obsessive sexual infatuation is the way it distorts our sense of self and boundaries. When we are in the throes of intense attraction, we often neglect our own needs in the hope that we can merge with the other person and become whole through them. This is where the concept of **boundaries** becomes essential. Boundaries are the invisible lines that protect our sense of self. They help us to define where we end and the other begins, and they serve as a safeguard against losing ourselves in unhealthy dynamics. A boundary can also be a guideline or limit that we intentionally set up and share with someone we're in a relationship with, letting them know that pushing it will harm us.

Identifying our boundaries, especially in the heat of passionate desire, can be challenging. Often, boundaries are only noticed when they've been crossed: when we feel violated, overwhelmed, or emotionally drained. This is why it's vital to cultivate awareness before, during, and after intimate encounters. If we don't know what our boundaries are because we haven't had a lot of relationship or sexual experience, self-reflection can be an excellent tool.

After an encounter—whether it was physically intense, emotionally charged, or both—take time to check in with yourself. How do you feel? Do you feel whole and energized, or do you feel depleted, anxious, or conflicted? If the latter, it may indicate that your boundaries were not respected, either by you or by the other person. Do you feel like you were dosed with dopamine and you need another hit? This may be veering into sexual obsession. The more we practice self-reflection, the more we learn to tune in to the subtle signals of our own discomfort and misalignment.

Journaling can be a particularly effective tool in this process. Writing about your feelings, desires, fears, and emotional triggers can help you track patterns over time. What are the circumstances that trigger obsessive feelings? How do you respond to those feelings? Do you tend to lose yourself in them, or can you create space for them without becoming consumed? This process of writing helps to bring clarity to the confusion and can shed light on the deeper, unconscious forces at play in your relationships.

Another essential tool in navigating obsessive sexual infatuation is the practice of **detachment**. Detachment doesn't mean shutting off emotions or disconnecting from love; rather, it is the ability to remain emotionally grounded and centered while still being open to love and desire. It's the art of experiencing attraction without being swallowed by it, feeling deeply without losing your sense of self in the other person. Detachment is about recognizing that your worth is not dependent on another person's attention or approval, and that true love never requires you to abandon yourself.

This practice of detachment is often challenging in the midst of intense encounters. In those moments, the rush of connection can feel like a lifeline—like the only thing that matters. But when we are swept away by desire, we risk losing our ability to act in alignment with our authentic selves. Detachment provides a counterbalance to this tendency. It allows us to remain clear-headed, to recognize when our boundaries are being compromised, and to choose to step back when needed.

Working with a therapist or trusted spiritual guide can also be a powerful tool in navigating these intense dynamics. A therapist can help you unpack the underlying causes of obsessive sexual infatuation, such as unresolved childhood trauma or unmet emotional needs. They can also support you in recognizing

patterns of sexual compulsivity, where the compulsion to seek out sexual experiences becomes a way to numb emotional pain or fill a void. Therapy provides a safe space for you to explore your triggers, your desires, and your relationships to both sex and intimacy, allowing you to understand and heal the root causes of your behaviors.

Sexual compulsivity in particular is a serious and often misunderstood issue. It is not simply about seeking pleasure; it is about seeking a sense of relief or escape from emotional pain through sexual encounters. This cycle of relief and craving can be particularly difficult to break, as it involves deep emotional and neurological patterns that are reinforced by the temporary satisfaction of physical connection or having sex again. Breaking free from sexual compulsivity requires not only understanding the root causes but also committing to a path of healing that addresses both the psychological and physical aspects, without letting anyone shame you for your feelings.

Finally, one of the most important tools for navigating obsessive sexual infatuation and compulsivity is **self-compassion**. This is perhaps the most difficult, yet most necessary tool for the process. When we are caught in unhealthy cycles, whether in a sexual context or otherwise, it is easy to fall into shame or self-blame. But healing begins with the recognition that we are not broken or defined by our mistakes. We are whole, and we are deserving of love, not despite our struggles, but because of them. Self-compassion allows us to approach our healing with kindness and patience, acknowledging the pain while also believing in our capacity to heal and grow.

As we navigate the complexities of intense sexual encounters, obsession, and compulsivity, it's crucial to remember that the journey is not about perfection. It is about understanding, self-awareness, and creating space for growth. It's about reclaiming our sense of self and our boundaries, so that we can experience love and intimacy from a place of wholeness, not neediness. Only through this process of self-discovery and healing can we create space for truly healthy, balanced relationships—ones that honor both ourselves and the other without pathologizing our need for pleasure.

The Make-Up Sex Cycle

As in the example of Nick and Claire, it's very common for Twin Flame couples to have outrageous fights. These aren't typical fights about who did the dishes last night (although when mundane fights do happen in Twin Flame relationships, they often escalate and end up being about something else entirely). When Twin Flames fight, you can almost see the sparks of rage in the air. After all, when you fight with your Twin Flame, you're fighting with your own shadow-self; the intensity is unmatched.

But if these fights are legendary screaming matches that feel like the end of the world, they can also end up inspiring some of the hottest, wildest, most intense and loving make-up sex afterward. It's as if lifetimes of love and desire

are unleashed when Twin Flames have sex after a fight. But often, this make-up sex cycle never gets to the root of the conflict.

Whether you're trying to figure out if your current, active, reciprocated relationship is a Twin Flame relationship; are working through an unrequited love for someone and want to understand why you feel what you feel; or are experiencing repeated bouts of rage and make-up sex with your Twin Flame lover, it can be helpful to get a sense of your own attachment style, which we'll explore in Chapter Six.

* * *

5

FACING THE SHADOW TOGETHER

The "shadow" is a concept across cultures that's been around for many centuries. It was first used as a psychological term by psychoanalyst Carl Jung, a disciple of Freud. It's a concept that can help us better understand the parts of our psyche that are repressed and unseen.

Put simply, the shadow is the part of us that we're afraid to face. And that's why working with it is so powerful: because facing it, processing it, and accepting it can help us to integrate and heal our whole self. This increases our self-esteem and helps us in our relationships, making us better able to self-validate so we're not constantly looking to our partner for approval. When we're not battling or hiding our shadow (from ourselves and others), we also have more energy and general enthusiasm for life.

Freud believed that our psyche is divided into an id (the part of our subconscious that is pure, unbridled instinct and desire) and an ego (the part of us that we show to others, because we deem it to be socially appropriate). Jung believed that this battle between the id and the ego in childhood—stifling the "bad stuff" you've repressed in favor of the "good stuff" that society applauds—forms the shadow, which remains with us for our entire lives, until we integrate it. If the ego is the manicured lawn of the psyche, the shadow is the deep forest just beyond the backyard.

Carl Jung and Jungian Theory

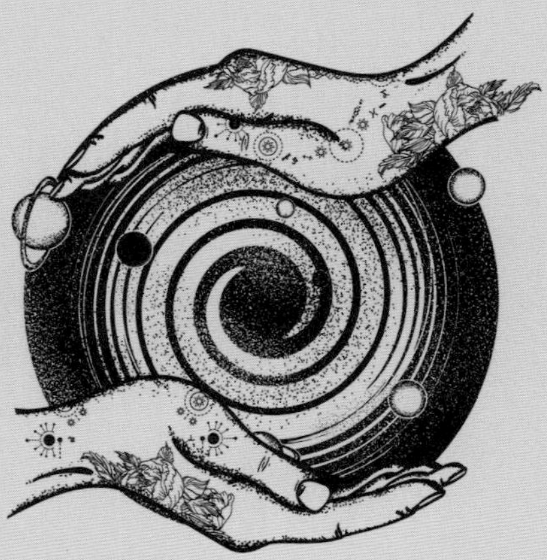

To understand the Twin Flame concept (or for that matter, any modern psychological model of the soul), it's essential to explore the work of Carl Gustav Jung (1875–1961), the Swiss psychiatrist, depth psychologist, and visionary thinker whose ideas shaped much of what we now call shadow work, inner union, and spiritual individuation.

Jung broke with his early mentor, Sigmund Freud, not just because he wanted to widen the frame of psychoanalysis, but because he couldn't accept Freud's insistence that all psychic life must be rooted in materialism and sexual repression. Jung was willing to walk into the mystical woods, to listen to the symbols that came through his dreams, and to sit at the crossroads of science and spirit without needing either to dominate the other. This set him apart, both in his own era and in ours.

What made Jung so radical wasn't simply his theory of archetypes or the collective unconscious, but his claim that the soul was real, and that we could engage it. For Jung, the psyche wasn't just a structure of cognition and behavior. It was a living field of symbols, drives, and ancestral echoes. The unconscious wasn't something to be "fixed" or overwritten—it was a mystery to be explored. And it had its own intelligence.

His notion of the *collective unconscious* posited that we carry more than our own personal experiences. We inherit mythic patterns and primordial images—what he called *archetypes*—that structure the way we experience the world. These include figures like the Mother, the Hero, the Trickster, and crucially for our purposes, the Anima and Animus. These latter two represent the internalized opposite-gendered aspects of the self. Though these terms are dated in their binary language, they were Jung's attempt to articulate how we hold both masculine and feminine energies within us, regardless of gender identity or sexual orientation.

Jung believed that the people we fall in love with often carry projections of these inner archetypes. We don't just see them as they are; we see them as manifestations of our deepest longings, fears, and unconscious drives. This is the psychological skeleton key to many Twin Flame relationships: We are drawn not just by who the other is, but by what our soul recognizes in them. Jung didn't use the phrase "Twin Flame," but his framework of projection, shadow, and soul work has informed nearly every New Age or psychospiritual model that uses that term today.

In fact, Jung is often unwittingly cited when people speak of "mirroring" in these relationships. The idea that another person can reflect your unhealed wounds, your unmet needs, your unlived life, stems directly from Jung's belief that everything unresolved within us will eventually appear outside us in our relationships and context. As he wrote, "Until you make the unconscious conscious, it will direct your life and you will call it fate."

One of Jung's greatest contributions was the concept of "shadow work," a term now widely used (and often watered down). For Jung, the shadow was everything in us that we disown—our rage, jealousy, power, sensuality, vulnerability—all that we exile to make ourselves socially acceptable. But these rejected parts don't disappear; they wait underground until they are triggered. And when we meet someone who activates our shadow, it can feel as if both ecstasy and terror are unleashed. The Twin Flame bond, in its most intense form, can force these disowned aspects into the light. Whether this results in healing or destruction often depends on the level of consciousness brought to the dynamic, and the work we're

willing to do to get there. Jung also emphasized *individuation*, which he defined as the process of becoming one's whole self—not by becoming perfect, but by integrating all parts of the psyche. This is not self-improvement; it's self-encounter. The goal is not to become someone else, but to become fully oneself. For those recovering from or reckoning with Twin Flame experiences, this is crucial.

In the later part of his life, Jung delved deeper into alchemy, Eastern philosophy, astrology, and the I Ching—not because he believed in superstition, but because he saw in these systems symbolic representations of the psyche's journey. He was deeply interested in synchronicity—meaningful coincidence—and believed that the soul communicates through such events. Synchronicities are often reported by those on the Twin Flame path: strange meetings, dream visitations, and so on. Jung's framework invites you to interpret these as messages from the unconscious—not predictions, but invitations to pay attention.

Though some of Jung's language now feels outdated, particularly his gender essentialism, his work remains a cornerstone for anyone attempting to bridge psychology and spirituality. He refused to reduce human experience to neurosis or pathology. Instead, he invited us to see our suffering as meaningful, our dreams as revelatory, and our love stories as sacred texts written by the soul.

Psychological Projection

One of the most common issues that comes up in Twin Flame relationships (and one that can be directly addressed using shadow work) is psychological projection. Projection, in the psychoanalytic sense, refers to the unconscious act of attributing one's own feelings, thoughts, or traits to another person, especially when those aspects of ourselves are difficult to accept. It is a defense mechanism—one that serves to protect us from confronting the parts of our psyche that we may deem unacceptable or shameful. In relationships, especially those as intense as Twin Flame connections, projection becomes a powerful force that distorts reality and creates conflict, often without either partner realizing the deeper dynamics at play.

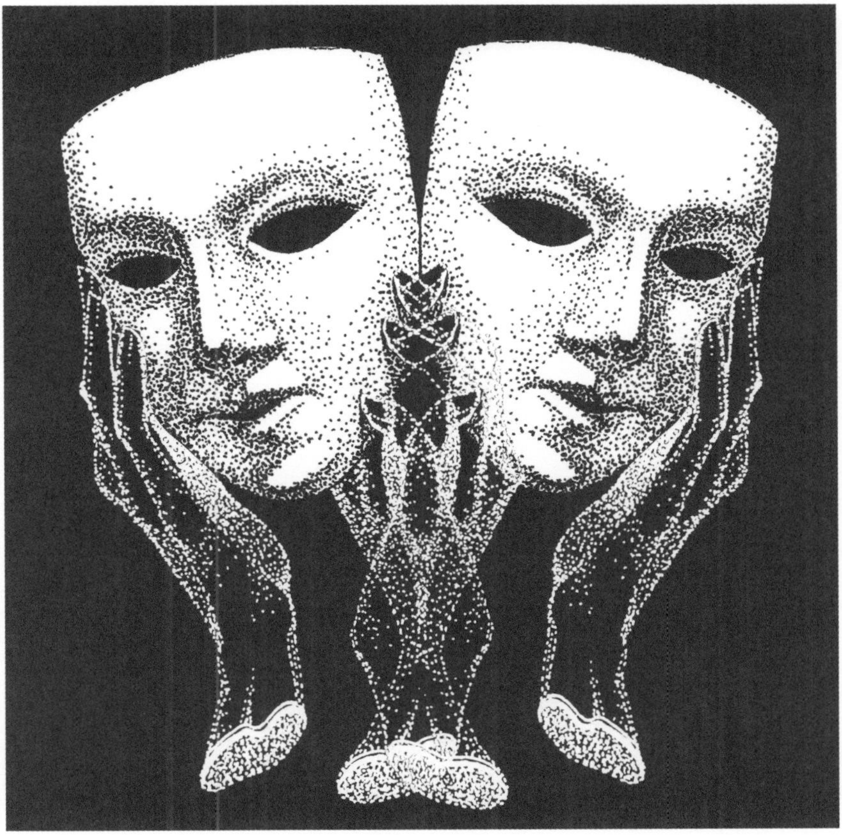

For instance, in a romantic relationship, one partner may project their own insecurities about intimacy onto the other, accusing them of being emotionally distant or unavailable. But the truth is, the projecting partner is the one who struggles with vulnerability and fear of abandonment. By projecting these feelings onto their partner, they are able to externalize their internal struggles and avoid confronting the pain that lies beneath. In doing so, the projection creates a cycle of misunderstanding and emotional distance, as the partner who is being projected upon begins to internalize the accusation, perhaps feeling defensive or guilty for something they never intended.

Another common example of projection occurs when one partner, overwhelmed by their own unhealed wounds, projects their fears of betrayal onto the other. Perhaps they are afraid of being left behind, and so they accuse their partner of flirting with others or entertaining emotional connections outside the relationship. The fear is real, but the accusation is not. It is an internal battle being fought outwardly, and it often leads to resentment and mistrust between the two partners.

What Is EMDR?

EMDR, or Eye Movement Desensitization and Reprocessing, is a therapeutic modality developed in the late 1980s by psychologist Francine Shapiro. Originally designed to treat post-traumatic stress disorder (PTSD), it has since been used to address a wide range of psychological wounds, including anxiety, depression, attachment ruptures, and relational trauma. Unlike traditional talk therapy, EMDR doesn't rely on verbal analysis alone. It's based on the premise that the body and brain can process traumatic memory when gently guided through bilateral stimulation—usually through guided eye movements, tapping, or auditory tones.

The core insight of EMDR is that trauma doesn't live only in the past—it lives in the nervous system. Unprocessed memories can get stuck, looping in the background like an app draining your battery. These memories aren't integrated; they remain emotionally charged and frozen in time. EMDR allows the brain to unfreeze and reprocess these experiences—not by erasing them, but by placing them in a coherent narrative that no longer feels like a threat in the present.

In an EMDR session, the client focuses on a specific traumatic memory while simultaneously engaging in bilateral stimulation. This dual attention appears to mimic what happens during rapid eye movement, or REM, sleep, the phase when the brain naturally processes and integrates emotional material. As the memory is activated and metabolized, it often loses its emotional intensity. The goal is not to forget, but to remember differently: to recall the event without being retraumatized by it.

For those recovering from emotionally charged relationships—especially Twin Flame dynamics marked by high conflict, abandonment, or gaslighting—EMDR can help break the spell of looping thoughts and reactive attachment patterns. It works directly with the limbic system, where trauma resides, allowing for resolution without needing to retell the story endlessly.

What makes EMDR especially powerful is that it doesn't require full intellectual understanding to work. It bypasses the overactive mind and meets the body where it already remembers. It honors the intelligence of the psyche—trusting that when given the right conditions, we are wired to heal.

Projection in Twin Flame dynamics is particularly potent. Because the bond is often so intense and mirrors our deepest vulnerabilities, projections can fly unchecked, magnifying both the shadow and the light within each partner. One person might project their unhealed wounds onto their Twin Flame, blaming them for their pain instead of owning their part in the emotional entanglement. It can become a battle of projections, each partner accusing the other of things they themselves fear, until they confront the truth that they are not seeing the other clearly, but through the lens of their own projections.

The process of recognizing projection involves deep self-awareness and a willingness to confront the parts of ourselves we avoid. Only by acknowledging these projections can we begin to break the cycle and embrace the truth of who we are, and who our partner truly is.

Working with the Shadow

There are so many different ways to work with the shadow, including psychoanalysis with a trained Jungian practitioner; art therapy; Eye Movement Desensitization and Reprocessing (EMDR); self-driven shadow work like active imagination (more on that later in this chapter); dreamwork; journaling; and likely many more. If you're currently embroiled in a Twin Flame relationship, or are in the wake of one that's ended, doing shadow work individually can be essential to understanding and healing that relationship. Always start with yourself before moving toward doing shadow work with a partner. Once you're in better touch with the nature of your own shadow material, it should be easier to work with the wounds and projections that come up in your relationship.

Twin Flames and Shadow Confrontation

Some people go their entire lives without confronting their shadow. This might be because they've repressed that part of themselves so deeply—often due to early childhood or generational trauma—that the wall they've built to hold back their shadow is impenetrable. You might think this means they're happy campers, as they avoid dealing with anything "dark," but that's definitely not the case. It takes tremendous energy to repress the shadow. Doing so can keep us from ever knowing what we truly desire and what would give us real, authentic happiness. Conversely, integrating our shadow parts can foster creativity and a sense of aliveness. Understanding and accepting this part of ourselves allows us to claim our erotic power: Not only does it feel good, it can provide us with the kind of magnetism that other people can't help but notice.

The goal of shadow work, according to Jung, is to achieve "individuation," which is a process of reintegrating our shadow, bringing it out into the light of our consciousness. This process beautifully mirrors the experience of meeting a Twin Flame, because the triggers we experience in these relationships show us the parts of ourselves that we don't always want to look at. When a soul that was split in two confronts its other half, it faces parts of itself that it excised in

a previous lifetime. It makes perfect sense that confronting your Twin Flame bears similarities to doing individual shadow work. Partners in Twin Flame relationships might be understood not just as two halves of one soul, but as parts of a shared consciousness that appear to one another as the shadow: both scary and alluring. It might feel like their "other half" is constantly showing up as their shadow, forcing them into confrontation with the part of themselves they have shunned.

And yet, each individual partner in the Twin Flame relationship is also a whole human. If you aren't ready to face *your own shadow*, you are going to struggle with your Twin Flame. But no one can force you to do this work before you are ready, and it's okay to do it on your own timeline—even if that means ending your Twin Flame relationship because it's too much, too soon. No matter the benefits of shadow work, we are each entitled to choose for ourselves when and how we engage with the parts that we've run from or repressed. If you're not ready to make peace with those parts of yourself, however, sustaining and healing a Twin Flame relationship will likely prove particularly challenging.

Shadow work isn't a spell, and it doesn't guarantee an easy path forward. But if you're in a Twin Flame connection—a catalytic, soul-shaking bond where your deepest fears and desires get projected onto another—shadow work often doesn't feel optional. This kind of relationship will drag every unloved part of you into the light, often through the mirror of your partner's behavior. That might just be the whole point, and it's where the healing begins.

One of my favorite tools for starting with shadow work is active imagination. Active imagination isn't daydreaming; it's a Jungian alchemical playground—a portal where your conscious self meets the dreamers, tricksters, or wounded witches living in your unconscious.

How to Use Active Imagination

Active imagination, one of Jung's essential teachings, is not just a tool—it's a rebellion against the impulse to organize and sanitize the psyche, causing repression and splitting off of vital parts of the self. It helps us to calm our inner chaos and bring creativity forward. And when done regularly, it can change your life and rewild your soul, making deep dialogue with soul familiars possible. This

is a kind of radical inner intimacy, a flirtation between the "you" you perform and the "you" you've buried—and perhaps the "you" that your Twin Flame has come to bring out.

STEP ONE: Enter the Liminal Space

With a journal nearby, find a space that invites quiet sensuality and safety. Light a candle, tune in to your breath, and ask gently:

"Who wants to speak to me today?"

You might meet an archetype (The Lover, The Crone, The Father), a shadow-self (A Jealous You, A Rageful You), or even a childhood version of yourself still clutching unmet needs.

STEP TWO: Engage the Dialogue

This is the part where your pen becomes a connection to the divine. You write the conversation between your conscious self and the figure who arrives. There is no censorship or logic. Let the voices speak—even if they shock you. Ask them questions. Let them ask you questions. This is a kind of soul-theater that might be erotic, or raw, or painful. Ask the archetypes, "Why are you here?" Listen to what they tell you and write it all down. This can help you remember that every part of you has a voice, even the ones you've exiled.

STEP THREE: Stay with the Tension

Don't rush to fix, explain, or banish what arises. Jung called this the "transcendent function"—the erotic charge of staying in conversation with opposites long enough for something new to emerge. (I'm using the word *erotic* here to draw your attention to a spark that makes you feel alive, not

necessarily something that causes you to feel sexually aroused.) Maybe your perfectionist meets your inner hedonist. Maybe your cynical self dances with your buried mystic. Ideally they don't cancel each other out; they become something else entirely.

STEP FOUR: Anchor It in the Real

Active imagination is only as powerful as your willingness to integrate it—to walk through your day carrying that inner figure beside you, not behind you. Finish up by writing about how the experience felt in your body and set an intention for how you'll use this new knowledge in your everyday life, how you'll embody it in your day-to-day reality.

If the sexual side of your relationship is the part that's causing you to encounter your shadow over and over again, or if the desire element is what's driving your relationship to toxicity, you might want to focus on a different kind of shadow work: the explicitly erotic kind. Getting more deeply in touch with your own desires is necessary so you don't project your authentic needs onto your partner (externalizing your inner desires instead of experiencing them) or become so enmeshed with their needs that you forget your own exist.

Healing through Shadow Work

A Twin Flame relationship will drag every unloved part of you into the light, often through the mirror of your partner's behavior. Doing shadow work is part of how we start to heal, even if it feels painful at the start. It's important to remember that you don't use shadow work to *fix* the other, but to **disarm the war within yourself**. This is the only way to stop reenacting that inner conflict in our relationships with others.

As you start doing solo shadow work, you'll begin to notice patterns and projections in your relationship. Now you can try to name those projections before they become a pattern. In Twin Flame dynamics, you often experience an irresistible pull accompanied by intense conflict, ghosting, obsession, or power reversals. This is not just trauma reenactment: It's shadow play that you aren't in control of. Identifying the ways in which you might be projecting your inner conflict onto your relationship with your partner helps you take your power back.

Ritual: Meet Your Erotic Shadow

This ritual is designed to evoke your erotic shadow, explore desires you may have repressed, and un-shame any parts of you that you may have hidden, because your family, culture, or society deem them unacceptable.

What You'll Need:

- ★ A private space where you can feel everything without censoring
- ★ Pen and paper or journal (no typing—you need the tactile magic)
- ★ An object that feels sexy to you, one that stimulates your primal self. This could be something you find in nature, like a rock or a stick, or even a vibrator, French Tickler, or silk scarf.

STEP ONE: Prepare a Sacred, Private Space

Set the scene as if you're summoning a forbidden lover—because you are, and it's you. Play music that you can feel in your pelvic region. Use scent to evoke eroticism: a vanilla candle or musky essential oil should do the trick. Breathe slowly. Let your breath dip into your pelvis. Drop out of your mind and into your body.

STEP TWO: Invitation

On the top of your page, write:
"I invite the part of me that wants what I'm not supposed to want."

Close your eyes. Ask silently:
"Who wants to speak to me? Who have I kept in the dungeon of my desires?"

You might see an image, hear a whisper, feel a sensation that doesn't make logical sense—just let it happen.

It could be:

- ★ The one who loves to be chased but never caught
- ★ The one who wants to be worshipped, not liked
- ★ The one who *loves* being too much
- ★ The one who is anything you can imagine it to be—sense into whatever comes up for you

STEP THREE: Dialogue

Now, write a two-way conversation between you and this erotic shadow. Let them speak freely. Ask them:

- ★ What do you want me to know about you?
- ★ What are you here to protect?
- ★ What turns you on that I keep shutting down?
- ★ What would happen if I let you lead, even just for one night?

STEP FOUR: Integration

To seal the ritual, anchor it. Choose one small, embodied act that honors this erotic shadow to complete in the next 24 hours. Some examples are:

- ★ Wear something that makes you feel untamed
- ★ Say something out loud you would usually silence
- ★ Dance without inhibitions
- ★ Bring yourself to orgasm
- ★ Tell someone what you actually mean, not what you think they want to hear

SARAH AND AMANI

Sarah and Amani stayed closely in touch through war and global conflict, even when they saw the stories of those events in different ways.

After Amani's family moved back to Lebanon in 2003, everything between them got quieter. September 11 cracked something open; not just geopolitically, but personally. Sarah, still in the US, was protesting in the streets against the impending war in Iraq. Amani, suddenly surrounded by checkpoints when she visited her family, started questioning their parallel histories. They were mostly on the same side: Both wanted peace and justice for all peoples in all the conflicts of the Middle East. Yet the small differences in their worldviews sometimes created large ruptures.

They sometimes fought over headlines and American assumptions, and, the impossibility of having a perfect friendship inside a wounded world. But even when they were angry, they still found each other.

In their late twenties, after two years of light contact and long silences, Amani came back to the States to visit cousins who still lived in Chicago. She and Sarah met in a coffee shop that had been a bookstore when they were teenagers. The city felt different, and so did they.

That night, without really planning it, they did a past life regression reading. What came through was unexpected. They weren't lovers in any of those lifetimes. They weren't sisters. In each one, they were protectors—inverting roles across time, shielding each other through plague, persecution, and war.

They cried afterward. Not out of sadness, but recognition. They had not been imagining it: Their shared trauma was not just individual, ancestral trauma, but soul-memory trauma.

Today, they live on opposite sides of the world. Amani married and moved to France to be close to her husband's family, and Sarah pursued her doctorate in Chicago. They do not talk every day, but when they do, it is like a soul check-in. Their relationship is still one of deep love and sisterhood.

Some Twin Flames are meant to teach you how to hold contradiction, and some are meant to teach you that love can stretch without breaking, across continents and centuries, and maybe even heal the world in the process.

If your partner triggers your trauma, ask yourself:

- ★ What quality am I assigning to them that I disown in myself?
- ★ Is their aloofness a mirror for my own fear of intimacy?
- ★ Is their hot-and-cold behavior echoing the way I abandon my own emotional needs?

The goal isn't to excuse their behavior—it's to take back your projections so you can respond from the core truth of who you are, not from the wounded part of you that might still be reactive and self-protective.

Interrupt the Abandonment-Narrative Loop

Shadow work shows us that many of our behaviors are defenses against early emotional injury. The Twin Flame relationship activates these wounds with surgical precision. Before you send the 3 a.m. text, or freeze them out for not anticipating your needs, pause and ask:

- ★ Am I responding to the present, or to an old story of betrayal?
- ★ What part of me feels abandoned right now? And who originally abandoned that part?

Tend to that inner exile first. Only then can you reenter the relationship as an adult, not a frightened child in a lover's body.

Own Your Shame, or Be Owned by It

Twin Flames often expose our most tender parts, including jealousy, possessiveness, or a craving to be chosen—and with that exposure comes shame. Shadow work is the antidote to self-rejection. As in the exercises throughout this chapter, you can try writing to the part of you that feels too much: that raw, wounded part of you that entered into a Twin Flame relationship unhealed. Ask:

- ★ What are you protecting me from?
- ★ What do you wish I would say instead of hiding you?

When you integrate these shadows, you stop needing your partner to hold them for you. You can show up in love without requiring constant reassurance or control.

Dismantle the Savior Myth

Shadow work requires us to let go of the fantasy that the Twin Flame will complete us. That belief is seductive but rooted in lack—the belief that we are not enough on our own—and lack is a magnet for chaos.

Ask yourself:

- ★ What am I hoping they'll rescue me from?
- ★ What part of me still believes I'm not enough without them?

Healing means letting the connection *inspire* your evolution, not outsourcing your wholeness to their presence.

Make Peace with the Mirror, Even If They Can't

Sometimes your Twin Flame is doing their work; sometimes they're running from it—and you can't control that. But you can decide what to do with the reflection they offer. Shadow work teaches you to stay present with what's real, not just what seems romantic in the moment. It prompts you to ask:

- ★ What does this relationship reveal about how I love?
- ★ Can I hold the mirror without needing it to be perfect?
- ★ Am I ready to love them without losing myself?

That's the alchemy of shadow work within Twin Flame relationships. You become the flame, not just the twin. Healing a Twin Flame relationship isn't about manifesting a reunion; it's about becoming so intimate with your own shadow that you stop playing out unconscious scripts. If they return, you meet them from wholeness. And if they don't, you still get your life back.

* * *

6

TOXIC TRAUMA AND ATTACHMENT STYLES

From trauma triggers to toxic rage, there are many different patterns and problems that arise in Twin Flame relationships. In fact, people often realize that they're in a Twin Flame relationship and not a conventional relationship *because* it evokes deep, complicated, and challenging layers of trauma. When you're in a relationship with your Twin Flame, someone with whom you once shared a soul, you might find yourself constantly challenged and provoked by your partner's words and deeds.

The good news is that we can learn to communicate about what hurts and cope with it openly and compassionately. This can take a lot of work, reflection, and even guided therapy—both individual and couples therapy—but the reward just might be that you and your Twin Flame grow together, not apart.

Trauma Triggers

The word *trigger* has become so overused in our culture—from people posting TRIGGERED memes in online arguments to people saying "Stop triggering me" to anyone who annoys them—that it's easy to forget what the term actually means. Triggering goes beyond "I don't like what you're doing." When you're truly triggered, it's because someone unexpectedly touches a wounded part of you, causing you to relive past trauma. In Twin Flame relationships, this happens a lot, in both directions.

It might be something as simple as your partner forgetting to pick up the dry cleaning that you told them you need, and you fly into a rage when they return without it. It's not about the clothes that you wanted to wear, of course, because you can probably just grab something else out of your closet. It's more about *not being heard* and what that brings up for you from your past.

An emotional trigger in a Twin Flame partnership isn't always as innocuous as in the example above. Jealousy is a very common Twin Flame trigger, because the fear of being abandoned by your partner brings up the initial soul-splitting you experienced in a previous lifetime. So, if your partner has a relatively harmless tendency to flirt with waitstaff in restaurants, this could send you off a cliff. Or if they return home late from work without texting you, or if their ex likes one of their Instagram posts, you might erupt in anxiety and rage.

What connects *anger over the forgotten dry cleaning* to *jealousy about your partner leaving you for someone else* is that there is usually a pattern that stems from your past. And with a Twin Flame relationship, the word "past" is more complicated, because we're not only talking about your childhood where you struggled to be heard by one of your parents, but about the previous lifetime(s) when your soul was entwined with that of your Twin Flame partner.

And even if the pattern began in this lifetime, it's not always possible to trace it back to its source. Sometimes you can unwind the remembered experience from childhood, but sometimes that memory is nowhere to be found, and you must learn to accept your emotions and work through them. One of the tools for navigating these emotional patterns is called *attachment theory.*

What Is an Attachment Style?

An attachment style is your soul's early choreography for closeness. It's how your nervous system learned to reach for love or brace for its withdrawal. It's the blueprint etched in your emotional body from your earliest bonds, long before you could name what you needed. Whether you were raised by your biological parents, adoptive or stepparents, or another kind of guardian, the way you were held and protected in your earliest life is part of the matrix that shapes the way you seek and give love as an adult.

Attachment theory came out of postwar schools of psychology. British psychoanalyst John Bowlby began mapping the tender terrain of mother-infant bonds. His colleague Mary Ainsworth created the *Strange Situation* study. In it, they watched babies seek safety, flinch from its absence, or fall silent in its wake.

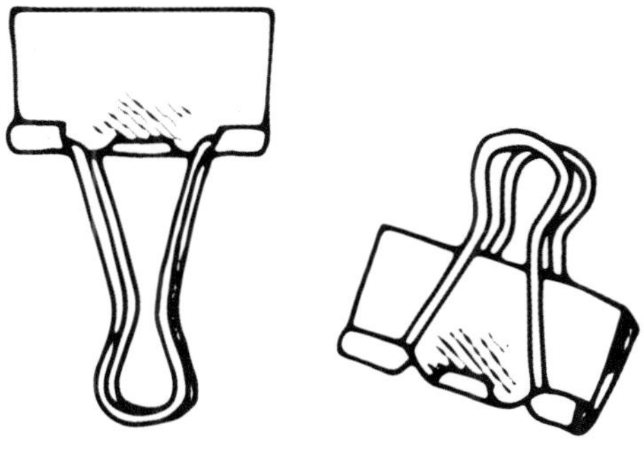

The Four Main Attachment Styles

1. Anxious Attachment

The one who aches for closeness.

People with anxious attachment long for intimacy like a desert craves rain—passionately, impatiently, desperately. Love is a high-stakes game of "Will they stay?" and "Am I enough?" Their heart is wired to hypervigilance, often misreading silence as rejection and space as abandonment. This is a very common attachment style for at least one of the partners in a Twin Flame relationship.

Sexually, they may fuse desire with validation. In bed, they're often generous, attuned, and eager to please, hoping that devotion between the sheets will guarantee devotion outside of them. But when intimacy becomes performance, it leaves them depleted. They often confuse being wanted with being safe. For them, sex can be a yearning for union.

2. Avoidant Attachment

The sovereign soul who guards their heart.

Avoidant attachment types value autonomy and treat vulnerability like a loaded weapon, alluring but dangerous. Relationships feel like a tightrope between craving connection and fearing engulfment. They may keep lovers at arm's length, constructing emotional safety with distance and detachment.

Sexually, they might be incredibly magnetic and skilled in the art of seduction, yet wary of the intimacy it brings. Physical connection may feel safer than emotional closeness, so sex becomes either a controlled performance or a compartmentalized act. After an orgasm, they may pull away—emotionally, physically, or both—protecting the fortress of their solitude. Their sexuality is confident but often disconnected from their deeper emotional needs.

3. Disorganized (Fearful-Avoidant) Attachment

The paradox in motion.

Disorganized attachment style craves closeness but trembles in its presence. Raised on a diet of mixed signals or emotional volatility, they learned to associate love with unpredictability. They oscillate between pulling a partner in and pushing them away, often confused by their own needs.

Sexually, their expression can be intense, charged, and sometimes chaotic. They may crave sex for intimacy one moment and use it to avoid it the next. Desire is mixed up with fear; arousal may coexist with dissociation. Their erotic life can be thrilling but unstable—a mirror of their internal conflict. Healing for them means learning to feel safe in their own body, not just someone else's arms. This is another common attachment style we find in Twin Flames.

4. Secure Attachment

The lover at peace.

They approach relationships with trust, emotional fluency, and self-respect. They know that closeness doesn't require self-erasure and that independence doesn't mean isolation. They communicate needs clearly, set boundaries compassionately, and invite others to do the same.

Sexually, they embody presence. They can surrender to pleasure without losing themselves, and they honor both their desires and their limits. For them, sex is connection, not currency. It's an act of mutual exploration, not negotiation. Whether slow and sacred or wild and playful, their sexuality is grounded, an extension of emotional safety rather than a substitute for it.

In the 1980s and beyond, researchers like Mary Main, Phillip Shaver, and Cindy Hazan applied the theories developed in response to this research to adult romantic relationships. (A word of warning: Many pop psychology takes on attachment styles are deeply heteronormative, using tropes like "needy women" chasing "emotionally unavailable men," as if the psyche runs on outdated rom-com tropes; take such gendered generalizations with a hearty helping of salt.) Attachment theory posits that your early childhood experiences shape how you love, how you long, how you leave—or how you stay even when you shouldn't. The model offers some useful metrics in assessing the nature of your relationships, including Twin Flame relationships.

Your attachment style influences:

- ★ How you ask for connection
- ★ How you process intimacy and conflict
- ★ How safe you feel when fully seen, especially when naked (emotionally and literally)

Attachment styles aren't fixed. They shift as you unlearn, as you heal, or as you meet partners who don't mistake distance for independence or devotion for desperation. Don't be discouraged if you discover that your attachment style isn't serving you—take it as an opportunity for curiosity and growth.

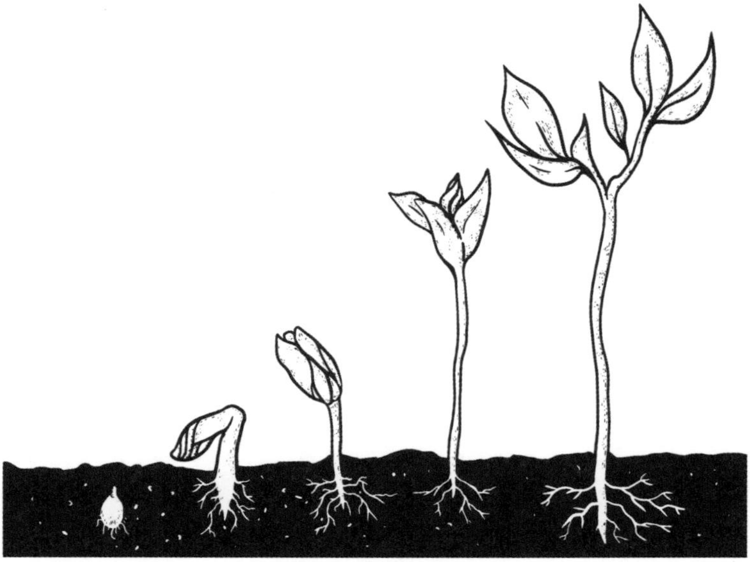

Romanticizing Toxic Behaviors

One of the most vexing problems in the online discourse around Twin Flames is the way that toxicity in these relationships can be romanticized, encouraging people to stay in abusive relationships. Those seeking advice are sometimes told to "stick it out" because they're in a once-in-a-lifetime relationship, and they should wait for their partner to realize how good they have it. This is terrible, dangerous advice that can get people hurt. It's okay to leave any relationship, even a Twin Flame relationship, because the most important thing for all of us is to be safe.

If your partner has ever been verbally, mentally, or physically abusive, never tell yourself that it's okay because your souls are linked. In fact, people often mistake a run-of-the-mill toxic relationship for a Twin Flame partnership, because there is so much emphasis on trauma and turmoil in the popular discourse on the subject. It's also possible to use the idea of Twin Flames to repeat trauma from early childhood, especially if you were lacking in healthy experiences of love or never got your needs met.

But Twin Flame relationships, like any relationships, can become harmfully toxic and abusive. And because they can escalate so quickly, it's important to be aware of the typical patterns that exist early in a relationship with an abuser. The early signs of a toxic or abusive relationship are not always obvious—they tend to masquerade as intensity, romance, or "chemistry." But underneath, they're bids for control, signs of emotional instability, or strategies of manipulation beginning to unfold.

Here are some red flags that may surface in the first few weeks or months of a toxic relationship:

Love-Bombing

- ★ Over-the-top affection, gifts, or declarations of love *very* early on
- ★ Phrases like "I've never felt this way before," or "I can't live without you" within days or weeks of meeting
- ★ May feel flattering at first, but it's often a tactic to fast-track emotional dependence

Moving Too Fast

- ★ Pressuring you to commit quickly (for example, asking, "Why do we need to date other people?" on a second date)
- ★ Wanting to move in, merge finances, or talk about marriage extremely early
- ★ Creating a false sense of urgency around the relationship

Boundary Testing

- ★ Pushing physical, emotional, or time-related boundaries and brushing off your discomfort
- ★ Guilt-tripping you when you ask for space or alone time
- ★ Showing up unannounced, texting constantly, or acting possessive of your schedule

Jealousy Disguised as Passion

- ★ Getting upset when you talk to or mention other people, especially exes or friends
- ★ Constant "checking in" that's framed as caring but feels invasive
- ★ Trying to isolate you from others ("Your best friend doesn't really seem happy for us")

Subtle Criticism or "Negging"

- ★ Jokes or comments that undercut your self-esteem, often followed by "I'm just kidding; you're too sensitive"
- ★ Correcting how you dress, talk, eat, or express yourself
- ★ Making you feel like you're lucky to be chosen by them

Mood Swings and Emotional Volatility

- ★ Intense highs followed by unexplained coldness, withdrawal, or rage
- ★ Feeling like you're constantly walking on eggshells, unsure what version of them you'll get
- ★ Using emotional reactions (sulking, silent treatment, tantrums) to control the dynamic

ALEX AND SIDNEY

After working together for just one day, Alex and Sidney both knew something unstoppable was building between them. They stayed late at the office that first night and as they rode down in the elevator in the empty building, they kissed for the first time. The electricity was so overwhelming that Alex wondered if they'd short-circuit the elevator and get stuck in there all night. (She kind of wished they would.)

But after the first few weeks of their intense affair, Alex knew that it was messing up her life. She felt addicted to Sid—to the visceral chemistry of their physical connection and the mind-blowing sex they were having on the sly. She would pretend to leave the office to go home after work, only to dash into the train and take it two stops to meet him in a hotel. She was spending so much money on her babysitter that she wasn't paying her electricity bill. She'd often miss the last train home and have to Uber in order to be home by midnight. She was feeling enormous guilt about missing her kids' bedtime several nights a week.

Sid's girlfriend became suspicious within days, and after a week, she confronted him. Sid had fallen so madly in love with Alex by this time that he told his girlfriend the truth. She moved out that night.

Alex and Sid's work relationship was also a tumultuous one. They both had strong personalities. At first, Alex found Sidney inspiring and Sidney thought Alex brilliant; their creativity sizzled when they were in the same space. But they also argued. Loudly. In the office where others could hear. They would scream and slam doors and even though the conference room was supposed to be soundproof, everyone heard them yelling.

After three weeks, Alex could no longer keep claiming that she was working on a special project when her kids asked why she hadn't been around to tuck them in. Her ex-husband and her babysitter were both asking a lot of questions, because her kids kept saying "Mommy stays so late at work." Her colleague Greg confronted her at work, saying her fights with Sid were creating tension in the office. He was ready to fire Sid and report Alex to HR.

After this double-whammy reality check, Alex broke off her romantic affair with Sid and recused herself from his project, asking Greg to assign it to someone else so Sidney wouldn't get fired.

Sid was devastated, and so was Alex, but she knew that she had made the right decision for her mental health and her relationship with her kids. When it proved too painful to see each other every day at the office, Alex asked if she could work from home for a few weeks.

Getting some distance from Sid helped Alex clear her head and reset her priorities. She was able to focus on her household responsibilities and be there for her kids each night. She also reached out to her former therapist, a Jungian, and restarted their sessions. After just a few conversations, they realized that meeting Sid unleashed her anxious attachment and everything spilled out from there. She was able to address and heal childhood wounds (an absent father and overprotective mother) and understand her relationship with Sid in ways that were clarifying and deeply healing.

When it was time for Alex to return to the office, she called Sid and they talked it through. They agreed that, at least for now, they couldn't start sleeping together again. But they acknowledged the overpowering chemistry between them. Going out on a limb, considering they had only been involved for a few short, yet steamy weeks, Alex asked Sid if he'd be willing to do some couples counseling with her to get at the root of their intense connection. He agreed. Through this process, they learned how to communicate with each other without fighting, and the toxicity vanished.

By now, Sid had finished the project and was no longer working in Alex's office. They decided to try dating again, but without the secrecy this time. Although they still argued, they were able to get to know each other, learning each other's histories and traumas, and developing a loving, respectful way of talking things through. They remained in couples therapy, and Alex encouraged Sid to pursue individual therapy as well. Because Alex understood by this point that Sidney was her Twin Flame partner, together they also explored all manner of modalities to better grasp the nature of their past life together. Using hypnotherapy, past life regression, Akashic Records sessions, and other tools, they began to gain some insight into how and when they had previously known each other. Five years after meeting, they married and took a honeymoon on the island of Ios in Greece, where they had discovered they'd once lived, circa 2300 B.C.

And sweetest of all: The sex was still the best either one of them had ever had.

Victim Narratives

- ★ Sharing stories about "crazy exes" or how *everyone* has hurt them
- ★ Blaming others for all their past relationship problems and never taking accountability
- ★ Using past trauma to excuse toxic behavior, instead of owning healing work

Gaslighting

- ★ Dismissing your perspective or reinterpreting events to make you doubt your memory or judgment
- ★ Saying things like, "You're imagining things," or "That's not what I said," even when it very clearly is
- ★ Finding yourself apologizing constantly, even when you're not sure what you did

You're Already Anxious

- ★ You feel more emotionally off-center, anxious, insecure, or self-doubting than usual
- ★ Friends or family raise subtle concerns, and you feel defensive even though you're unsure why
- ★ Your body might know before your brain does: You notice an unpleasant feeling in the pit in your stomach, have difficulty sleeping, or experience a shrinking sense of self

Early-stage toxicity often hides in charm, flattery, and intensity. Abusive people tend to prey on those they perceive to have low self-esteem. If you're seeing these signs or even feeling that something's off, it's worth slowing down and checking in with yourself or someone you trust, like a friend or family member.

Communication in Twin Flame Relationships

Once you establish that you're not locked into an abusive relationship, it's time to address and unpack your trauma. Plugging into therapy is almost always a good idea for people in a Twin Flame partnership, because the constant triggers can be exhausting. And if you're working with a good couples therapist who can teach you how to communicate with each other with compassion, you'll be far ahead of the game.

7

ENDING THE RELATIONSHIP

Not all relationships are meant to last forever, but when Twin Flame pairings end, the pain is palpable. It's like having your organs torn out. Many people resist letting go, even if the relationship itself is mired in constant conflict. But how do you know when it's time to say a final goodbye (at least for this lifetime)?

You do not let go of a Twin Flame relationship because it stops mattering; the experience will be with you for the rest of your life. You may let go because it starts hurting more than it heals. You may let go because the mirror becomes a magnifying glass for your pain instead of a portal to your expansion. The signs are not subtle when it's time to leave, even if you have been gaslighting yourself for years.

You might find yourself constantly triggered and rarely soothed. Conversations that once felt electric now feel like emotional warfare. Instead of building something together, you feel like you are tearing each other down in both subtle and overt ways. Maybe your communication has gone from sacred soul-speak to walking on eggshells, with every word measured to avoid another meltdown.

You might feel like you're stuck in a loop where you chase and they retreat; then they chase, and you hide. The back-and-forth keeps you locked in emotional whiplash. It starts to feel like a karmic treadmill where you are running and running but never getting anywhere.

Most telling of all, if the growth has stalled and you're no longer expanding, you might know that it's time to go—especially if you're repeating the same lesson over and over again, and instead of evolving through it together, you are regressing. You might feel more anxious, less secure, and increasingly disconnected from your intuition, your joy, and your connection to your own erotic spark.

Letting go does not mean you've failed. In fact, it is the opposite. It means you've finally recognized that holding on was costing you too much. It means you were brave enough to stop betraying yourself. Letting go of a toxic Twin Flame relationship is not a rejection; it's more of a redirection back to yourself. It's choosing the version of you that does not need chaos to feel alive.

When it's time to go you get to choose your peace and your future. And sometimes, that means leaving behind a love that once lit up your entire nervous system. You'll never forget them because they changed your life and rewired your soul. And if you meet them again the next time around, in a new lifetime, perhaps you'll get to be together with less drama, and more healthy, bonded love.

NICK AND CLAIRE

For almost a year, Claire and Nick circled each other like moths to a flickering bulb, always drawn back in but never quite able to land without getting burned. They broke up over coffee in the East Village and got back together under the Williamsburg Bridge at sunrise. They had screaming fights outside art galleries in Chelsea and whispered apologies in bed, limbs knotted in sweaty forgiveness. Each time felt like the last, but it was not.

Then one day, Nick simply stopped answering. No blowout fight, no final email, no closure; just silence. Claire was gutted—not by his disappearance, but by how unsurprised she was. She realized she'd been bracing for it all along.

But the pain wasn't wasted. In the hollow space Nick left behind, Claire didn't collapse: she expanded. She started to see that Nick had been much more than merely a lover; he'd been a mirror, reflecting parts of herself she hadn't yet dared to meet. He illuminated her shadow: the part of her that equated longing with love, that mistook intensity for intimacy. He showed her how easily she confused emotional unavailability with mystery, and inconsistency with passion.

In the quiet that followed, she got to work: therapy, journaling, bodywork, and long solo dinners. She took a break from dating for six months and got to know her own body again. She stopped trying to be "the cool girl" who could tolerate bad behavior and started asking herself what love without adrenaline felt like. Slowly, she stopped craving the high. And in its place, she built a relationship with herself that wasn't performative, or curated, or conditional.

Years later, Claire is married to a man who doesn't trigger her trauma—he actively listens and holds her. Their sex is less volcanic and more oceanic: deep, steady, and surprisingly wild. Sometimes she thinks of Nick and smiles; not with longing, but with gratitude. He was the spark, but she lit the fire herself.

Why We Hold On Too Long

By now, this should be obvious: because holding our soul's other half in our arms, or knowing that they're near, can feel like nothing else on earth feels. It's validating, comforting, surreal, and divine to actually meet your Twin Flame in real life. And when there is sex involved, the obsessive, addictive qualities of the relationship can also be hard to resist.

It's fairly common for Twin Flames to come with an "I can't quit you" element that brings lovers back together over and over again, even when they know they can't live together in any real way. This can go on for months or even years, until one or both halves of the partnership realize that it must end. Sometimes, this is why Twin Flame relationships end in a ghosting or no-contact breakup. (If the drama and toxicity is impossible to contain, this can actually be a mature way to bring a relationship like this to its close.)

We might stay because we believe no one else will ever see us the way our Twin Flame partner did. The high of a Twin Flame relationship can feel sacred, and your body may remember the way your partner's breath rewired your nervous system. It can be hard to say goodbye when their eyes saw into you like no one else ever had. If you spoke in a soul-language, finishing each other's thoughts, dreaming the same dreams, and imagining a shared future, ending things with them can feel like cutting out your own heart on purpose.

That kind of recognition feels like lightning striking. Twin Flame chemistry is not just sexual, but alchemically activates every chakra, every trauma, every buried desire. It can feel like destiny intended you to be together.

If we know it's healthier to leave but we can't or won't, it may be because our abandonment wounds are quietly calling the shots. It may not feel like merely losing a limb or a vital organ; it can feel like cutting off access to God. Then there is the grief, often complicated by spiritual narratives. You may have told yourself that this person is your divine counterpart, your destined partner, your mirror flame. And so you stay, believing that any pain you experience is part of the sacred journey, telling yourself that if you just heal enough, stay patient enough, and hold on long enough, the pain will transmute into paradise.

But here is the truth: Soul recognition is not the same as soul compatibility. Just because someone reflects your shadow and your light does not mean they are meant to walk beside you for the rest of this lifetime. In some cases, they were your mirror, not your match. Maybe they were your catalyst in this lifetime, not your companion. And acknowledging that truth can set you free. It is not about erasing what you shared; it's about releasing the fantasy so that you can finally embrace the reality. Your healing does not have to include them and your expansion can happen without their permission.

The Death of a Relationship

Leaving a Twin Flame relationship can usher in an extended period of grief. Your friends or family might say, "It's just a breakup," but to you, it feels like a death—a tearing away of layers that were fused together in fire and longing and karmic threads. When a Twin Flame relationship ends, it can feel like a death because it is the end of a sacred contract. When you walk away from the person who reflected your deepest truths, or they from you, it can feel like a piece of your soul has been surgically removed. Because in a way, it has.

You are not just grieving the person. You are grieving the version of yourself that was forged in their presence. The dreams you shared, the life you imagined, and the texts you never sent. The love you gave without holding anything back. Losing those things often feels like the collapse of an entire world, and the loss is not just emotional; it's psychic and somatic. Your nervous system goes into withdrawal, aching for the energetic high that only they could bring (or so you believe).

You may find yourself disoriented and questioning your intuition. You may wonder if the entire connection was a lie. But if you've gotten this far and done the work, trust that it was your truth, at least for a little while. It was just not meant to last in the way you hoped. Give yourself permission to grieve the breakup like it was a death. It's okay to let yourself fall apart for a time and mourn what was and what could have been. Sit in the ashes of your fantasy until you can see the first glimmer of new growth. Because every death makes space for a rebirth you cannot yet see. And this one? It is about your resurrection. You are not being punished; you are being reforged.

Analyzing Break-Up and Make-Up Loops

Each loop of the break-up and make-up cycle teaches you something. Each return peels back another layer of illusion. If you are caught in this cycle, it is not your fault. But it is your responsibility to ask:

- ★ Is this reunion rooted in growth or fear?
- ★ Has my partner truly evolved, or am I clinging to a vision that doesn't exist?
- ★ What am I afraid to face within myself if I let them go for good?

Breaking the cycle is not the same as breaking the bond; you can honor the love while refusing the chaos. You can hold gratitude for what you shared while choosing peace over passion. When you walk away for the last time, it is not because the love was fake. It is because you finally understand that love without safety is not sustainable and chemistry without commitment can be a recipe for heartbreak. You do not owe anyone your suffering; you are allowed to walk away from pain, even if it once felt like a sacred calling.

The Break-Up and Make-Up Loop

The cycle is real in Twin Flame relationships that are on the decline. This intense push-pull dynamic can create a pattern that is both addictive and exhausting, where intensity masquerades as intimacy and longing is mistaken for love. And perhaps every time you've already walked away and come back, a voice inside you has whispered: What if this time it is different?

Maybe the make-up sex is electric. The apologies are poetic, and the promises feel like prophecies, so you go back. And for a moment, it feels like the divine reunion you always imagined—but then the cycle repeats.

Try not to beat yourself up if you've gone back more than once: You are human after all, and hope is a hell of a drug. Especially when it is mixed with karmic chemistry and spiritual storytelling of this magnitude.

Cutting Contact

Sometimes, the only way to survive the aftermath of a Twin Flame breakup is through silence. It may be that the bond between you is too intense and the pull is too strong for you to remain in contact. The energetic cord between you needs to be severed completely so you can heal.

It can be valuable to remember that people don't leave because they stopped loving someone. They leave because:

- ★ Their nervous system is fried. The emotional highs and lows have become unsustainable.
- ★ The growth has become one-sided. One person is evolving, while the other remains stuck.
- ★ They have become a version of themselves they no longer recognize. The relationship has distorted their sense of self.

In these moments, silence is not cruelty. It could be an act of sacred self-preservation. It may be that you're choosing your sanity over your storyline. Sometimes walking away with no apology must happen because staying would be a spiritual self-betrayal.

The Stages of Grief

One of the most profound lessons of the grieving process that people learn when they've lost someone, whether to a sudden or expected death or a breakup, is that grief is never linear. All the stages below might come in a different order for you, some phases might be more intense or overwhelming, and some might loop back around more than once.

1. **Denial:** You convince yourself they will come back. You replay every moment, searching for signs. You believe if you just send the right text, everything will go back to the way it was.
2. **Anger:** You rage against the universe. Against them. Against yourself for believing in the dream. You feel betrayed by your own heart.
3. **Bargaining:** You negotiate with God, fate, and yourself for one more chance, one more message, one more vision board of the future you were supposed to share.
4. **Depression:** The ache becomes a fog. You might lose interest in things that once lit you up. You may cry in public or stop believing in love. You could wonder if the pain will ever end. (It will.)
5. **Acceptance:** One day, you wake up and they are not your first thought. You realize you have gone hours without checking your voicemail, your email, and without secretly snooping on their social media. You can breathe without breaking. Now the air feels different, lighter.
6. **Integration:** You take the lessons and own your part. You finally forgive yourself and transmute the longing into power. You rise from the ashes with new wisdom, new boundaries, and a heart that is scarred but still open. You become the version of yourself that your soul familiar was sent to activate: You become your own flame.

Ghosting vs. Saying Goodbye

Ghosting is the easy way out, but sometimes it must be done. It might feel quick, clean, and painless for the one doing the leaving. But for the one left behind, it is a psychic cliff-hanger. It triggers abandonment trauma. It leaves questions hanging in the air like unanswered prayers. If it can be avoided, it should. Of course, if it's not safe to keep engaging, then by all means, cut off all contact.

Saying goodbye with presence is messier. It takes courage and means sitting with the discomfort of truth. But it offers closure to the person you're leaving and it honors the connection. It allows both people to move on with dignity.

When leaving becomes a necessity, the most important thing is that you actually do it. But if you can, choose presence over disappearance. You deserve to leave with your integrity intact. But what if you're the one who's been left? You'll grieve either way, and you should know what it might feel like.

* * *

8

TOOLS FOR REINTEGRATION

Before we look at ways to reintegrate after a Twin Flame relationship ends, or continue the healing process if our Twin Flame relationship is ongoing, let's revisit our three case studies to see where the Twin Flames in this book ended up.

Some of these relationships closed gently, some broke open, and others remain in motion. But none of them were clean and easy. None of them offered resolution without first demanding something raw and real from the people involved.

Claire and Nick couldn't find a way to stay together. Their chemistry was undeniable, but so was their instability. They looped through connection and rupture for a year, always circling back to each other but always ending up in the same place. When Nick finally ghosted Claire, she was left alone with more questions than answers. She searched for spiritual meaning in his disappearance, but what she found wasn't a cosmic justification. It was an invitation to tell the truth about the patterns she kept mistaking for love: that intensity and intimacy are not the same thing. And that a nervous system trained in unpredictability will often confuse adrenaline for connection.

Twin Flame connections don't deliver guarantees. They ask questions and strip away your ability to pretend you're fine with shallow love, false safety, or self-abandonment. They surface your earliest beliefs about worthiness and desire and devotion. They can ignite, yes; but they also expose. This path doesn't promise partnership; it promises awakening.

Chemistry Isn't the Compass

In the early stages of a Twin Flame relationship, the pull toward the other can feel like clarity. You recognize them instantly. Synchronicities build; you finish each other's thoughts. Your dreams speak to each other across time and space. Everything feels heightened, as if the universe is conspiring to show you something too big for language. And for a while, it works—until it doesn't.

This is because the same connection that opens your heart might also light up your fear, and the same chemistry that draws you closer might also retraumatize you. The body doesn't always distinguish between what's magnetic and what's destabilizing.

Sidney and Alex lived inside that paradox. What began as something hot and affirming quickly revealed the parts of themselves they had kept at arm's length: anger, fear of engulfment, and unmet needs they didn't know how to express. They both brought their unfinished business to the table and expected the other to carry it. But instead of collapsing under the weight of those expectations, they started asking different questions. Not, "Are we meant to be?" but, "What is this showing me about myself?"

They chose to find each other again, not because it was easy, but because they wanted to understand themselves better. They chose to keep seeing each other after a healthy break, showing up not just with their hearts, but with their whole histories. That's not the kind of love story we're taught to want. But it's the kind that transforms us.

The Mirror Isn't the Destination

It's tempting to believe that the person who activates something deep inside you is the one who's meant to stay. We're trained to assume that recognition means permanence and that soul contact should lead to romantic fulfillment. But Twin Flames don't always arrive to be our partners. Sometimes they show up to reflect the parts of ourselves we've hidden, rejected, or misread entirely. The mirror is powerful, but it is not the point.

Amani and Sarah's bond began long before either of them had language for it. As children, they moved through the world side by side—two girls shaped by different cultural legacies, tethered by a friendship that felt older than their current lifetime. For years, their closeness was seamless. But when the instability of the world interrupted them, they argued and misunderstood each other. But they never truly disconnected.

Years later, when they came together again with new tools and a shared willingness to go deeper, they shared in the experience of discovering their Twin Flame bond. The past life regression didn't solve the past; it gave them a wider lens. Their connection no longer had to exist in one particular form. It could stretch, change, make room for silence, and remain sacred. The intensity softened into something steadier—not less meaningful, just less fragile.

Modalities for Healing

There's no one-size-fits-all path for integration; healing is highly personal. But there are some tools that are well suited to healing the intensity of Twin Flame relationships. The following modalities are especially useful if a relationship has activated your nervous system or shaken your sense of self. They can support different layers of the healing journey:

- **Somatic Experiencing:** This body-based therapy helps re-regulate the nervous system and restore a sense of safety in your physical self. It's especially useful when the relationship triggered trauma responses.
- **Psychodynamic Therapy:** This modality explores childhood attachments and unconscious patterns that may have surfaced during the connection. It's a slower path, but powerful for rewriting internal narratives.
- **Parts Work/Internal Family Systems (IFS):** This kind of therapy is useful when you feel "split" between longing and logic. IFS helps you meet the parts of yourself that still cling to the fantasy, without shame.
- **Group Therapy or Support Circles:** Being witnessed in your experience, without needing to explain it, can provide profound validation and reduce isolation.
- **Grief Counseling:** Even when the person is still alive, Twin Flame endings can evoke complicated grief. Working with a therapist who understands ambiguous loss can be essential.
- **Energy Work or Reiki:** For those drawn to nonverbal treatments or seeking energetic clearing, these practices can support the release of attachment at a subtle level.
- **Body-Centered Practices (Yoga, Feldenkrais):** These modalities help recalibrate the body's responses to relational stress. They're especially useful if you held tension or trauma in specific areas of the body during the relationship.

Choose what meets you where you are. You don't have to heal the whole story all at once. You just have to start where it hurts.

Not all spiritual reunions look like romantic closure. Some look like forgiveness without performance. Some look like honoring the bond without needing it to behave a certain way. A Twin Flame mirror is never meant to mark the ending of one's journey. Rather, it lights the flame of our inner awakening, ushering us on a journey that not only lasts through this lifetime, but heals both the past and the future.

Spiritualizing the Wound

One of the more damaging ideas in Twin Flame discourse is the notion that all pain is divinely orchestrated and that any abandonment was meant to teach you; chaos was part of the plan. You often hear that the heartbreak came with instructions tucked inside it like a coded message from your guides.

But some experiences are just plain painful; not everything is sacred. And not every person who hurt you was sent to shape you. Claire spent a long time trying to assign meaning to Nick's disappearance. At first, she looked for signs, read too much into coincidences, and tried to make spiritual sense of his absence. But nothing about his behavior improved by calling it fated. What changed was her willingness to let go of the story that kept her small.

Healing didn't arrive through interpretation; it arrived when she stopped trying to decode it. When she stopped needing it to mean anything profound

Journal Prompts for Healing

- What did I believe love was *supposed* to feel like before this connection, and what do I believe now?
- Which patterns surfaced in this relationship that I've seen before in my past?
- What did this person reflect back to me about my shadow, my needs, or my boundaries?
- Where did I abandon myself in pursuit of connection, and what would self-loyalty look like now?
- What parts of me still believe that pain is a prerequisite for passion?
- When I close my eyes and visualize safety in love, what do I feel in my body?
- What would it mean to forgive, not them, but myself?
- Where does longing live in my body, and what soothes it?
- Who am I now that the mirror is gone?
- What kind of love would feel *easy*, and am I ready to receive that?

and accepted that the rupture didn't need to be mystical to be real, she was finally able to grow up and out of it. And when she learned about Twin Flames years later, it did add a new layer of meaning to the experience—but she had already learned what she needed to learn, and that was good enough.

What Love Feels Like

We don't talk enough about the fact that love can feel unfamiliar once it becomes safe. If you've spent years in survival mode—if your nervous system learned that desire must come with confusion or distance or shame—then calmness can feel like absence. You might misread steadiness as boredom or resist comfort because it doesn't match what your body has learned to

call connection. But real healing and shadow work changes the terms of recognition.

After Claire let go of the fantasy she had built around Nick, she stopped chasing emotional intensity as a stand-in for depth. What came next wasn't lightning and it wasn't an immediate spiritual revelation. It was a different kind of clarity—the kind that doesn't scream for attention. She stopped performing the version of herself that had once kept his interest. She learned what it meant to be chosen by someone who didn't need her to collapse herself in order to feel close.

Amani and Sarah's relationship remained deep and enduring. They had a shared knowing of not just their childhoods, but a soul memory that didn't require constant contact to feel alive with meaning. Sidney and Alex chose to remain together, but not through fantasy and drama. They chose each other because they wanted to, not because they believed they had to, or because their families approved. Claire moved on. She built a love she didn't have to chase. Each of them walked a different path. But all of them arrived at the same threshold: the space between identity and awakening, between longing and embodiment.

* * *

CONCLUSION

You may never reunite with the person you once called your Twin Flame. They may remain a part of your past, a closed chapter, or a name you stop speaking aloud. That doesn't mean the bond was false. It means the bond had a different purpose: that the point was never the person; it was what they activated within you. And if they do stay in your life, as they did for two of the pairs of our case studies, you're in for a lifetime of learning and reintegration. It's a profound path to choose.

Twin Flame connections are initiations. They ask you to feel what you haven't felt before, to face what you've been avoiding, and to remember who you were before you started trying to become what others needed. Some of these relationships end and some evolve. All of them invite you to become a new version of yourself along the way.

That is where transformation happens if you're one of the rare, lucky few to meet your Twin Flame in this lifetime—not in the reunion with the other, but in the return to yourself.

This book has invited you to examine the myth of Twin Flames, to question the narratives around them, and to understand their potential as both a catalyst and a crucible for personal growth. The Twin Flame journey is not a fairy tale. It is a path of deep, transformative, often excruciating change. It is a reckoning with self and other—a challenging, but ultimately liberating, passage through the heart of love and self-knowing. And perhaps, in the end, the greatest gift of all is this: that you will emerge, not as you were before, but as the person you were always meant to become. A version of yourself that is whole, awake, and free.

* * *

REFERENCES AND RESOURCES

Books

Flood, Gavin D. *An Introduction to Hinduism.* Cambridge University Press, 1996.

Hanegraaff, Wouter J. *New Age Religion and Western Culture: Esotericism in the Mirror of Secular Thought.* Brill, 1997.

Jung, Carl G. *Man and His Symbols.* Dell Publishing, 1968.

Kripal, Jeffrey J. *Esalen: America and the Religion of No Religion.* University of Chicago Press, 2007.

Porges, Stephen W. *The Polyvagal Theory: Neurophysiological Foundations of Emotions, Attachment, Communication, and Self-Regulation.* Norton & Company, 2011.

Web Pages

Aybar, Susan. "4 Somatic Therapy Exercises for Healing from Trauma." *Psych Central.* https://psychcentral.com/lib/somatic-therapy-exercises-for-trauma.

Encyclopedia Britannica. "Hinduism." https://www.britannica.com/topic/Hinduism.

Patheos. "New Age." https://www.patheos.com/library/new-age.

Porges, Stephen W. "Polyvagal Theory: A Science of Safety." *Frontiers.* https://www.frontiersin.org/journals/integrative-neuroscience/articles/10.3389/fnint.2022.871227/full.

Springer, Shauna H., Ph.D. "Polyvagal Theory: How Your Nervous System Works." *Psychology Today.* https://www.psychologytoday.com/us/blog/free-range-psychology/202203/polyvagal-theory-how-your-nervous-system-works.

The Jungian Center. "Jung on Active Imagination: Features, Methods and Warnings." https://jungiancenter.org/jung-on-active-imagination-features-methods-and-warnings.

IMAGE CREDITS

Cover
Twin Flame illustration © Ertostudio

Poster
Clockwise from top left: figures embracing © Anna Ilchuk/Shutterstock.com; koi fish © Kulikova Valeriya/Shutterstock.com; thundercloud © modisketch/Shutterstock.com; swans © Elena Pimonova/Shutterstock.com; trees © Sasha_Ivv/Shutterstock.com; bouquet © Pagina/Shutterstock.com; whales © intueri/Shutterstock.com;
Center: dharma wheel © Naman Kheria/Shutterstock.com

Interior
1, 3, 10, 22, 42, 52, 64, 84, 98, 110 (stars) © Salomi art/Shutterstock.com; 10, 22, 42, 52, 64, 84, 98, 110 (sun), 41 (hands) © venimo/Shutterstock.com; 7, 101 © Marzufello/Shutterstock.com; 8 © Enola99d/Shutterstock.com; 11, 73 © Homeshark/Shutterstock.com; 12 © bc21/Shutterstock.com; 13 (top) © VectorFlower/Shutterstock.com; 13 (bottom) © awank 13/Shutterstock.com; 17, 66 © intueri/Shutterstock.com; 18, 19 © Istry Istry/Shutterstock.com; 21 © mehediHI/Shutterstock.com; 23, 24, 67, 68, 109, 111 © knstartstudio/Shutterstock.com; 26, 86, 100, 113 © Alexander_P/Shutterstock.com; 27 © Drafts n Doodles/Shutterstock.com; 28 © Anastasiia Mikhailova/Shutterstock.com; 29 © Elka_Marina/Shutterstock.com; 32 © Kseniakrop/Shutterstock.com; 34 © Black moon/Shutterstock.com; 35 © Anastasy_helter/Shutterstock.com; 36 © Very_Very/Shutterstock.com; 40 © M7Studio/Shutterstock.com; 44 © OneLineStock/Shutterstock.com; 46 © cybermagician/Shutterstock.com; 47 © Kalinkina Maria/Shutterstock.com; 48 © Mukti10/Shutterstock.com; 49 © Nadia Murash/Shutterstock.com; 50 © The img/Shutterstock.com; 51 © Tsareva.pro/Shutterstock.com; 54 © Ekaterina Glazkova/Shutterstock.com; 56 © Prasetiadp/Shutterstock.com; 57 © svetabelaya/Shutterstock.com; 58, 69, 115, 117 © Ma Di/Shutterstock.com; 59 © I Made Sugianta/Shutterstock.com; 61 © Arina Ulyasheva/Shutterstock.com; 63 © MD.Riaz Parvej; 70 © Croisy/Shutterstock.com; 72, 118 © ekosuwandono/Shutterstock.com; 75 © Prozo/Shutterstock.com; 78, 99, 102 © Shamanska Kate/Shutterstock.com; 81 © Alina Aksjonova/Shutterstock.com; 82 © anvinoart/Shutterstock.com; 87, 105 © Trilisti/Shutterstock.com; 92 © Kseniya Parkhimchyk/Shutterstock.com; 93 © Vorobiov Oleksii 8/Shutterstock.com; 95 © ONYXprj/Shutterstock.com; 96 © wawritto/Shutterstock.com; 97 © Babich Alexander/Shutterstock.com; 104 © Alex Rockheart/Shutterstock.com; 106 © Miraniuk Olga/Shutterstock.com; 107 © MerciArtworks/Shutterstock.com; 108 © Palform Pics/Shutterstock.com; 112 © Umaporn Thoonkhunthod/Shutterstock.com; 120 © Leonid Zarubin/Shutterstock.com

ABOUT THE AUTHOR

Sabina Strauss is an author, astrologer, and relationship counselor in private practice who has lived and worked in Miami for the last twenty years. Her client work blends astrological energy mapping and sex coaching; she helps individuals and couples better understand the soul contracts their charts have created for them. Strauss writes about sexuality, psychology, and the stars, and her stories and forecasts have appeared in dozens of outlets. Her body of work is at the intersection of metaphysics and relational meaning-making. She derives profound joy from helping readers and clients heal from heartbreak.

INDEX